A LIFETIME OF TEACHING

Portraits of Five Veteran High School Teachers

ROSETTA MARANTZ COHEN

Teachers College, Columbia University
New York and London

Published by Teachers College Press, 1234 Amsterdam Avenue
New York, NY 10027

Library of Congress Cataloging-in-Publication Data

Cohen, Rosetta Marantz.
    A lifetime of teaching : portraits of five veteran high school
teachers / Rosetta Marantz Cohen.
        p.   cm.
    Includes bibliographical references (p.) and index.
    ISBN 0-8077-3096-3 (alk. paper). — ISBN 0-8077-3095-5 (pbk.:
alk. paper)
    1. High school teachers — United States — Case studies.   I. Title.
LB1777.2.C64   1991   91-8884
373.11′0092′2 — dc20   CIP

Printed on acid-free paper

Manufactured in the United States of America

97 96 95 94 93 92 91   8 7 6 5 4 3 2 1

To my sister, Paula

Here is A who is much more successful than B in teaching, awakening the enthusiasm of his students for learning, inspiring them morally by personal example and contact, and yet relatively ignorant of educational history, psychology, approved methods, etc., which B possesses in abundant measure. The facts are admitted. But what is overlooked . . . is that the success of such individuals tends to be born and die with them; beneficial consequences extend only to those pupils who have personal contact with such gifted teachers. No one can measure the waste and loss that come from the fact that the contributions of such men and women in the past have been thus confined, and the only way by which we can prevent such waste in the future is by methods which enable us to make an *analysis* of what the gifted teacher does intuitively, so that something accruing from his work can be communicated to others.

—John Dewey, *The Sources of a Science of Education*, 1929

Contents

Acknowledgments

I would like to thank Professors Karen Zumwalt and Frances Bolin of Teachers College for their guidance and support throughout every stage of this study. I am also grateful to Samuel Scheer, Murray Cohen, and Cathy McClure for their ongoing suggestions and insights. I owe a special debt to the late Ron Galbraith of Teachers College Press, who edited this book with great sensitivity. Finally, I would like to express my gratitude to the following teachers whose example fostered in me a love and respect for the teaching profession: Mary Bentzlin, Ruth Marantz Cohen, J. D. McClatchy, Donald Justice, and John H. Moore III.

The completion of this project was aided by a generous grant from Trinity University.

1 Introduction

In my secondary methods class, at the start of every semester, I am in the habit of asking my students why they have chosen to become teachers. The first answers I get are nearly always either jokes or platitudes. "For the money," someone will say, or "Because teaching is spiritually rewarding." But when they press below the surface and really begin to reflect on why they are sitting in my classroom and not in a marketing class, an interesting phenomenon occurs. Invariably, the discussion turns to specific teachers, the one or two who left an indelible mark. All the students seem to have experienced at least one such figure who ended their somnolence, awakened them to a new way of thinking, or brought them a fresh appreciation of the familiar. Often they have not thought about these teachers for many years, but our discussion sparks their memories. Everyone ends up telling a story about someone "amazing" — the teacher who started it all.

What always strikes me, once this part of our discussion gets under way, is how the personalities and styles of the dozens of inspirational figures described are so radically different from one another. One student will speak of an adored elementary school teacher, the picture of maternal warmth, who turned every difficult task into a game. Someone else will describe a terrifying high school teacher whose bullying manner shook the student out of complacency. Some claim to have learned the most from teachers who afforded them extraordinary freedom, while for others it was a rigid taskmaster who ultimately left the deepest, most positive mark.

As a teacher of teachers, I was always interested in finding in these descriptions a commonality. I wanted to be able to say, both to myself and to the class, "You see, all these excellent educators had X, Y, and Z in common. All of them did this or did that, and this is why we remember them." Invariably, however, the actual stories confounded any attempt at drawing easy parallels. While all the remembered teachers were noted for their success at imparting information and for their love of their respective disciplines, it was obvious that their techniques, procedures, and personalities were anything but uniform. There were as many best-loved types as there were students recollecting them.

Once I realized to what extent the teacher and not the method was the cornerstone of a student's educational experience, it occurred to me that this was a lesson rarely taught in schools or departments of education. As a product of traditional methods courses, I myself have suffered the dismay experienced by most new teachers when they enter their first classroom. Little of what I learned seemed to apply to the real world. Being able to enumerate the four steps of effective classroom management, or knowing how to draw a bell curve of student test results, meant nothing in terms of my daily experiences. I didn't *feel* like a teacher. I felt like a catalogue of strange and curious information. What I wanted more than anything in those first, flush months in the classroom was a model, someone whose experiences might console or inspire me. I wanted to hear realistic stories about the specific difficulties of other teachers. I also wanted to see the larger picture, a perspective available only to a veteran professional.

One of the traditional justifications for the prescriptive and quantitative nature of nearly all preservice literature is that, for better or worse, this is what new teachers want. For years it has been assumed by professional educators that the novice is a concrete thinker, incapable of caring about anything more than basic survival. This was not true in my own case, and it does not seem to be true for the overwhelming majority of first-year teachers with whom I have worked. These teachers always seem to sense immediately the great limitations of prescription. Their complaint is not that they have not been taught the rules of good teaching, but rather that they have not been given a true picture of what good teaching, and teaching itself, are all about.

One reason for this is the limitations of student teaching. Very few student teachers ever get a chance to see great teachers in action. Another has to do with the paucity of literature, particularly on the secondary level, dealing with real classrooms and real people. Rarely does one hear a real teacher's voice in a textbook on secondary classroom methods, and lengthy ruminations by real teachers are virtually impossible to find.

The portraits in this book were written in response to that need. They are meant to fill a gap in secondary preservice literature by providing case studies with which real teachers can empathize and from which they can draw inspiration. These are stories of successful practitioners, told in their own voices and in the voices of those who have worked with them, lived with them, and sat in their classrooms. They are stories that ask the question: What does the life of a successful teacher look like?

The assumption behind this book is that the answer to that question lies in many subtle factors — in quirks of personality, in the childhood family, in the configurations of marriage and friendship. To understand the careers of devoted teachers is to know the first moment they fell in love with their subject, their worst argument with a colleague, their hobbies, and their medical problems. In teaching, as in few other fields, the life makes itself manifest in every aspect of the work.

These portraits also serve another function. They reinforce the lesson I learned from my students, that great teachers come in all styles, shapes, temperaments, and personalities. Nurturing or doctrinaire, sensitive or stoic, these teachers have all developed different and unique strategies that make their classes wonderful places in which to learn. There is a tremendous amount of professional wisdom shared in these pages, but it differs from personality to personality and from place to place. The goal of this book is not to quantify that wisdom. Rather, it is to show how practical wisdom in teaching is expressed through the particular experiences and idiosyncrasies of individual practitioners.

§   §   §

Individuality has never been celebrated or encouraged in the classroom teacher. Indeed, the earliest sociological studies of the profession depict the educator as a creature whose impulses toward self-expression had to be suppressed for the public good. Riding in cars, wearing makeup, even dating were all prohibited to teachers until well into the 20th century (Waller, 1932). It is not surprising, then, that residual forms of oppression should still exist. Today, top-down management continues to stifle imagination in the most gifted teachers. Recent legislation in states like Texas and Florida establish rigid and arcane mechanisms for evaluating public school faculty, such as the use of criterion checklists designed to reward homogeneity and penalize creativity. What talented person would choose to remain in a profession in which conformity and passivity are the most sought after and valued traits?

That question is ultimately answered by the teachers profiled here. Though they are candid about setbacks and disenchantments, about bureaucratic tyranny and the minute problems of everyday classroom life, these teachers also speak with extraordinary eloquence about the rewards of teaching, the strategies they have devised for circumventing oppression, and the reasons they have remained in the field. Their arguments contain no platitudes about "spiritual rewards." But their passion and their convictions about the profession are evident in every class these teachers teach, and in the way they live their lives.

THE SUBJECTS

Researchers interested in compiling life-history case studies generally begin their search for subjects with certain criteria in mind, criteria determined by the specific questions they hope to answer. Because the focus of this book is survival and long-term commitment, all the teachers profiled have taught for many years— at least 25 and, in three cases, for as many as 35 years. All five are survivors who have come up against adversity and then slipped past it with relative ease. What is more, all share a remarkable capacity for self-renewal, even when circumstances seem adverse to growth. They are all equally devoted to their work, even though that commitment plays itself out in decidedly different ways.

Four of the five teachers were discovered more or less through word of mouth. In every community, even the largest, the best teachers always seem to gain a kind of informal renown. Their identities are known, even to those not involved in education.

In searching for appropriate subjects, I asked for recommendations from students, colleagues, friends outside the profession, and parents with children in the schools. I made a point, however, of not asking principals or administrators for their recommendations. My fear was that their choices might be too conservative. I was not necessarily looking for the teacher who produced the highest test scores or for the one with the most school spirit. I was looking for the teacher who made the greatest impact on students' lives. That kind of teacher can sometimes be a gadfly, and not the favorite of those in charge.

The individuals who were ultimately chosen as my subjects were those whose memories of the past were most vivid, and whose candor about the profession and about themselves made them easy to talk to at great length. They were also the ones whose achievements both inside and outside the classroom were ongoing and impressive.

The first, Carl Brenner, has written several of the most popular math textbooks in use today. He has been a leader in national organizations for the teaching of math and is continually developing innovative techniques for math instruction and sharing them with colleagues. Andy Galligani has spent his career crusading for teachers' rights. A devoted mentor of new teachers and a fierce advocate of high standards, he is venerated in his community as a "very hard, but brilliant and inspirational" teacher. Lily Chin overcame both sexism and racism to become chair of a science department at a large inner-city school in south Texas. Her influential Engineering Club—created and sustained on a shoestring budget—has served to motivate some of the most disaffected students in her school, many of whom have gone on to the country's finest colleges. Bill Salerno has received much public recognition as a teacher. A runner-up for New York City's Teacher of the Year, he was awarded an honorary doctorate from Georgetown University for his outstanding work in the classroom, the first secondary teacher ever to receive that honor.

The last of the five subjects is my mother, Ruth Cohen, a 35-year veteran and my own most memorable public school teacher. Ruth Cohen took an undistinguished French program at a small suburban high school and transformed it into one of the most respected and rigorous programs in the state. She initiated the school's two Advanced Placement French courses and is sustaining student interest in them at a time when language enrollments are on the decline.

Admittedly, making one's own mother a subject for research and scrutiny is a risky business. There is the pitfall of bias and the risk of learning unpleasant truths. I also discovered, in my own case, a curious resistance to limiting and defining my subject, to isolating key traits and analyzing them with dispassion—all necessary operations when making a case study. The story of a parent is packaged and tied less easily than that of a stranger.

Despite these difficulties, however, I decided to include Ruth Cohen among my portraits because she so perfectly exemplifies the kind of individual this book celebrates. A veteran teacher who personifies excellence in the classroom, she has had a profound and enduring impact on her students.

THE METHOD

Though the portraits in this book differ in a number of ways from those found in traditional reports on anthropological fieldwork, I nonetheless call them "ethnographic." As it is used here, *ethnography* refers to a methodological intention, an attempt on the part of the researcher to enter into the world of the subject. The traditional stance of the ethnographic researcher is that of a participant observer who acts as a member of the society he or she is attempting to understand and document. Participant observers integrate themselves into the daily routines of the subject, questioning, hypothesizing, searching for patterns and causes, and analyzing their own responses to what is observed. Unlike the quantitative or process-product researcher, ethnographers are not concerned with forming generalizations or making predictions. They are concerned, instead, with getting down what exists, with creating a window onto a piece of ongoing, idiosyncratic, real-life experience.

What makes the case studies in this book ethnographic is that they are based on these concerns and have been built up using many of the tools of the cultural anthropologist. Each portrait is the product of intensive, open-ended interviews in which the subject often dictated the focus and direction of the talk. As in traditional ethnography, the portraits are meant to show their subject from many angles at once. Spouses, friends, students, and professional associates all speak within these pages, sometimes repeating stories already told by the subjects themselves. Like the traditional ethnographic researcher, I immersed myself in the culture of these teachers' schools — sitting in classes, taking notes like a student, hanging out in faculty lounges and cafeterias. It is often pointed out by educational researchers that a specific phenomenon is colored by the complex bureaucracy that surrounds it. I therefore tried to penetrate the bureaucratic rituals of roll-taking and pep rallies and to understand how state mandates filter down to the departmental level. Documents, including letters from former students, supervisors' recommendations, speeches, personal statements, and old lesson plans, were also used to construct a picture of the teachers' lives. The ethnographer works on the assumption that nothing is trivial, that every gesture has meaning in the context of some pattern yet to be discovered.

Discovering that pattern was the next step. As in other efforts of this kind, the portraits were constructed on a model of grounded theory. In this model, analysis and data collection alternate. The researcher gathers information in the field, scrutinizes it, and then forms a preliminary theory. Armed with this theory, the researcher returns to the field to test it. There it is discarded, modified, or expanded by more data. Again, the researcher pulls back and analyzes, forming yet another theory that must be validated.

By applying this iterative method to these case studies, I established a final hypothesis that explained the professional commitment and endurance of my subjects, their capacity to remain fresh and invested over so long a period of time.

I also refer to these case studies as *portraits*. I use that term in the sense of an artistic rendition, something drawn or composed with an organizing aesthetic in mind. Throughout the writing of these portraits I could feel the researcher's eye competing with the storyteller's. As researcher, I was concerned with factual accuracy; as storyteller, I wanted to document a kind of metatruth, an intuitive sense of the subject that inevitably transcends fact. My concerns as a portraitist were with nuance, inflection, and suggestion, all quite different from the ethnographer's stress on what was said or done.

While this artistic perspective is not common in qualitative research, it is certainly not unique. One finds it eloquently demonstrated in the work of such researchers as Sara Lightfoot (1983), who turns her artist's eye on the American high school and paints portraits of institutions that seem to breathe with life. Lightfoot defends the portraitist's stance in ethnography by analyzing the nature of artistic sight. The painted or written portrait, she explains, illuminates parts of the subject about which the subject may not be aware. "Portraits make subjects feel 'seen' in a way they have never felt seen before, fully attended to, wrapped up in an empathetic gaze" (p. 5).

From time to time throughout these portraits, my subjective eye surfaces. Qualitative research of this kind never pretends to be wholly free from bias. Indeed, it seems inherent in the nature of the methodology that the researcher's voice and vision should make themselves manifest to some extent. As Sara Lightfoot and others have explained, the subjectivity that is inevitably present in ethnography can be seen in positive terms, as an enriching factor, rather than in negative ones. In order to successfully identify with another person's perspective, one must be able to experience and reflect upon one's own (Lightfoot, 1983).

I hope these portraits do indeed exemplify the "empathetic gaze" described by Sara Lightfoot. The hours I spent with Ruth, and with

Lily, Bill, Andy, and Carl, were enriching ones, and I came to feel deeply about them and about the lonely battles and private victories they have known. The real and hard work of the teacher is too often hidden from public view. This book is, above all, an attempt to make public and to celebrate the lives of five fine teachers and what they accomplish every day.

2   Carl Brenner

The halls of Alamo Heights High School in San Antonio, Texas, have the clean, insulated feel of an old-fashioned high school—a school of the 1940s or 1950s, where students move from class to class in well-behaved clusters, gossiping about homecoming balls and basketball heros. School campaign posters line the corridors ("Wilson for Class Secretary—The Way to Go" and "Vote Clark for a Better Tomorrow"), along with ROTC placards and ads for class rings.

On the second floor, in the north wing, half a dozen students wait out the last seconds before the warning bell, lounging against the green asphalt walls. There is a conspicuous mix of types here: athletes in oversized jerseys and crew cuts; blond girls in tube skirts, plastic bracelets, and huge earrings in the shape of Texas, cacti, or 10-gallon hats; hispanic students in T-shirts and stone-washed jeans. "Is this Mr. Brenner's room?" I ask.

"The one and only," says a gigantic jock in immense Nikes, motioning me in with a flourish.

Inside the classroom, Carl Brenner shuffles through a mountain of papers on his desk by a far wall. Several students look on disconsolately. "Your tests are here somewhere," he says. "I'll find them later." The students linger, unconvinced. "I promise they'll turn up," he says. "Let's start. Let's start." He scatters them away like birds, with the back of his hands. "Good morning, ladies and gentlemen," he says, changing his voice to an incantatory singsong.

"Good morning, Mr. Brenner!" recites the class in unison.

"And so," he says grandly, "let the algebra class begin."

§   §   §

Carl Brenner, according to innumerable sources and in the words of one of them, is "the most famous math teacher in the state of Texas." As the author of four nationally adopted textbooks and keynote speaker at countless national conferences, Brenner (along

9

with Heloise of "Dear Heloise" fame) is one of San Antonio's most important celebrities. Brenner's home, a gigantic turreted structure in an affluent city subdivision, is testament to his worldly success.

But to his students and ex-students, and to the colleagues and administrators with whom he works, worldliness seems to be Brenner's least apparent characteristic. He is described by them as many things — brilliant, boyish, intensely enthusiastic, frustratingly disorganized — but nothing in their description suggests the prima donna. "Carl just loves to teach," says a colleague. "He loves it, plain and simple. The other stuff — the textbooks, the celebrity — they're all there in the background, but it's not who he really is."

§   §   §

Carl Brenner's education laid the groundwork for an academic career. The son of a successful engineer, Carl spent many of his formative years in Great Britain, where his father had been transferred as chief engineer in a machine-tool company. Public schooling in England proved to be far more rigorous than anything Carl had experienced before, or would experience subsequently. "I got over to Great Britain in the sixth grade, and already my contemporaries had done algebra and French. They were starting geometry and Latin. In the sixth grade! In England, once you start a subject, you keep going with it; so by the 12th grade you have 17 subjects — grammar, composition, literature, writing. During my 4 years in English school, I did 4 years of algebra, 4 years of geometry, 2 years of Latin, 2 years of trig, 4 years of French, a year of physics, and 2 years of chemistry. Students are pushed much harder over there."

When Carl returned to the United States, administrators at the high school in Floorsville, Texas, were confounded about where to place the ninth-grade prodigy. "The principal said, 'Show me what you know.' So I did some algebra problems for him, spoke a little French, and he said, 'Fact is, we have nothing to teach you, except maybe some Texas history.'" As a compromise, Carl was placed in the 12th grade, where he took English, Spanish, and "a lot of things I already knew."

From Floorsville High School, Carl went on to Trinity University in San Antonio and then, having decided on an engineering major, he transferred after a year to the University of Texas at Austin, where the engineering department was considered exceptional.

None of Carl's teachers or professors, either in England or the States, in high school or college, seemed to have left any particular mark on him. The role of mentor, and professional inspiration, would go to a man Brenner encountered after graduation, when he enlisted in the navy. When Brenner speaks about Hyman G. Rickover, it is with a mixture of reverence, ironic detachment, deep affection, and reserve. Rickover is the first person Brenner mentions when he speaks about his life. The story of Carl's career, as he tells it, is punctuated by quotations and anecdotes by and about Rickover, even though the last time he saw Rickover was over 25 years ago. "My inspiration for going into teaching," says Brenner, "really had a tremendous amount to do with the admiral.

"When I got out of college with my engineering degree, I took the Officer Classification Battery Test. Rickover, it seems, was looking for bright young engineers to work with nuclear submarines—designing, constructing, and testing them. He'd take a young man, maybe an ensign, and put him in charge of a whole department with all kinds of high-ranking officers below him. A commander would be reporting to an ensign, or a senior engineer at Westinghouse reporting to a young college grad who could say to him, 'Fix this, this, and this, or you lose your government contract.'"

Rickover took a strong liking to Brenner on the day of his interview. "His style of interviewing was infamous—very rigorous, even cruel," Brenner recalls. "He was looking for people he could work with, people who were poised enough to deal with their superiors and sharp enough to deal with the concepts." Brenner had heard stories of people forced to field a barrage of questions while sitting in chairs whose front legs were 6 inches shorter than the back ones. Others had been sent on absurd escapades to prove their resourcefulness. (For instance, "Come in Monday with a picture of yourself on top of the highest naturally occurring place in Washington, DC, and you've got the job. Go on! Out!") "My interview," says Carl, "was on Saturday. Everyone who worked for Rickover worked on Saturday because he did. It was automatic. He kept me waiting for a couple of hours, and when he finally called me in, I put out my hand but he wouldn't shake it. 'Sit down in that chair,' he said. 'How old are you?' 'Twenty-one.' 'What day were you born?' 'June 14, 1939.' 'What hour?' '10 P.M.' 'How do you know?' 'My mother told me.' 'How do you know she wasn't lying to you? How do you know she's your mother?!'"

Brenner claims that he got the job that day because he had the gumption to stand up to Rickover, to get angry at him and talk back. It was the toughness beneath the deference that he thinks impressed the admiral.

Throughout his 4 years in the navy, Brenner developed a kind of reserved friendship with Rickover, whose office was directly across the hall from his own. The admiral was extremely interested in Brenner's British schooling. An advocate of the English educational system, Rickover would call Brenner into his office at regular intervals to testify before a variety of visitors to the rigor of his classes in the British public schools. "He made me aware of the terrible shortcomings of an American education," Brenner says.

The admiral, according to Carl, was also responsible for teaching everyone who worked for him how to write. A fanatical perfectionist, he required consistent clarity and simplicity in everything his staff put down on paper. "His theory was, 'If anything can be misunderstood, it will be,' a kind of Murphy's Law of writing. What was amazing is that Rickover read every letter written by every engineer in his department — every *draft* of every letter, every day — usually within a few hours of when it was written. Every secretary was required to send a pink copy directly to Rickover. He would catch things that were unexpected and always surprising. You would think you said something clearly, and lo and behold, it wasn't clear at all.

"Rickover inspired me in so many ways. He inspired me by being so conscientious, so directly oriented towards what he was doing. I have always had a tendency to get sidetracked, distracted. He taught me, in a harsh way, not to be lazy."

Brenner could easily have stayed on in the navy as a GS12, a high-ranking civil servant. Navy pay at the time was two and a half times a starting teacher's salary. But Rickover's education talk and his own brief experience as a high school tutor convinced Brenner that teaching would be an even more fulfilling career. With the admiral's blessing, he returned to college to be certified in secondary education.

"I guess I went in with a chip on my shoulder," Carl says of his Texas A & M coursework, "because I'd heard such things about education courses. But basically, what I heard was true. They were awful. In an adolescent psychology class, for example, if you memorized the subheadings in the book, you would do fine. There was absolutely nothing to learn in that class. And the teacher — if you watched him, if you mimicked him, you wouldn't last a day in a real classroom."

With that meager training, and with no student teaching experience, Carl went forth to find a job as a chemistry teacher—
the subject of choice for a former chemical engineer. "The fact is,"
Carl explains, "I had a very low regard for math when I was going
through school. I saw it as simply a tool for me to use for other,
important, things like science. I wanted to teach chemistry, physics
as a second choice, and math as a distant third." But when a math
job at Alamo Heights High School came along, Carl decided to take
it, having exacted a promise from the superintendent that the next
chemistry opening would be his. Several years later, when a chemistry position became available, Carl no longer had an interest in it.
By then he had developed a fascination and respect for math that
would stay with him for the rest of his career.

"My first brush with mathematics was in engineering," Carl
says about his transformation into a math lover, "and at that time I
had complete disdain for anything theoretical. I was only interested
in the applied. That was the only thing that was relevant. When I
got into the navy, we were working on problems that had never
been worked on before. You couldn't look up the formula. You had
to go back to fundamental principles. That laid the seeds for my
becoming a converted mathematician. When I started teaching
math, I realized more than ever how that subject underlies everything. Math is the foundation. It's beautiful and essential. . . . How
could I not want to teach the one thing you need to know in order
to be able to do everything else?"

§   §   §

It's homework review time in Carl Brenner's second-period algebra class. "21, 22, 23, 24," Carl scrawls the problem numbers up
on the board with a flourish. "Who wants 21?" he asks. "Who wants
23?" Students volunteer, then saunter with ninth-grade self-consciousness up to the blackboard to work out their equations. "David,
do number 24."

"I didn't volunteer," whines a young man in the back with elabo-
rately tied sneakers.

"You moved your shoulder. If you move your shoulder at an
auction, you've bought a piano." Accepting this reasoning, David
moves to the blackboard. "Remember," Brenner says, "all algebra is
just evaluating expressions or solving equations. I give you the answer, you give me the equation. Or I give you the equation, you
give me the answer. Simple! Simple!" The banter keeps up while

problems get worked out grudgingly on the board. "Okay," says Carl, "okay, let's see what we've got. What do you think of number 21, class?"

"Could you do it another way?" calls out a student. "Could you put the 120 on top?"

"Could you, class?"

"Yes!" the class calls out in unison.

"Convince me!" says Carl, and 25 voices shout back a barrage of alternative approaches.

"Now here's something interesting," says Carl, moving to the next problem. "Tamara's going to be a good mathematician because she's a lazy good-for-nothing." He pauses long enough to let this irony penetrate. "Good mathematicians are lazy good-for-nothings in that they try to do things in the easiest way they can. Look how Tamara skipped steps and made her answer as simple as possible." Carl writes out the intermediate steps in the solution as several students assiduously copy them down. "Could you do it another way?" asks Carl.

"Yes!" yells the class.

"Convince me!" says Carl. And the exchange continues.

§   §   §

"When I first started teaching," Carl says, reflecting back on the evolution of his style, "I asked a lot of questions, but it wasn't because I really wanted to know the answers. I'd ask a question if I wasn't sure how to teach something, as a way of sort of covering myself. Then I went through a phase where I knew the stuff too well. I just started telling the class. I knew all the answers so I would just steamroll over the class. Now, it seems, I've gone back to the way I was in the beginning. But for different reasons. Not out of insecurity, but out of confidence. I try to elicit questions, try to get it out of them. The first change in my teaching style happened because I knew the material too well. The second change, to my present style, happened because I knew it even better—knew it well enough to understand that there's no one right way. Now I'm constantly changing; I'm constantly letting the class change the way I view a problem. It's a much more creative and vital approach."

The longer Brenner taught, the more his approach took on the force of an ideology. His notion that "math is personal," that it is something one must "find out" how to do, was contemporaneous with the much-championed, and then much-vilified, principles of New Math. "The New Math really *was* theoretically on target," Brenner says. "The old way, the traditional way, said, 'Here's the formula. Here's five examples. Plug in the numbers. Find the answer. Pass the test. Forget it.' The New Math wanted students to understand the concepts *behind* the formulas. The problem was that New Math came from the top down. Professors made up this new approach, then handed it to teachers and said, 'Do this!' The professors assumed the teachers would teach the theory, then make up their own problems for the students to do by way of example. But the teachers only taught the theory. They never focused on the practical applications. All understanding and no technique. And it fell apart."

In 1972, more than 10 years after the New Math fiasco, Carl began writing the first in a series of math textbooks designed to correct the mistakes in what he was convinced had been a fundamentally right-minded approach. "In the traditional textbook," says Carl, "everything is broken down into disjointed little units. You do this page today, that page tomorrow. Each one is a little itty-bitty thing with no connection to what preceded it or to the real world. I knew in my bones that was not the way to teach. Even though I'd been taught that way myself." Brenner's approach is to reject the "itty-bitty" problems in favor of a few big ones in which a number of central ideas converge; in other words, to use problems that reflect the way math is used in the real world. "Because of my engineering background, it was easy for me to think of real-world applications — applications to bridges and buildings and baseball games. When students work my problems, they get an equation from which they can answer many questions instead of just one. They're using a *lot* of skills, and the focus is less on formulas and more on procedures."

§   §   §

Carl concedes that his method tends to appeal, when it is first introduced, to the off-beat kind of kid, the questioner. "The ones who would rather plug the numbers into the formula don't like this method. They get kind of scared. Some people have a mission in life to comfort the afflicted. I feel my mission is to afflict the comfortable. If they're comfortable using formulas, I say, 'Why? Prove it to me! Convince me!'"

"When I first found out I'd have Mr. Brenner," says Hallie, a former student, "I was petrified, even though I'd done well in math before. We all knew that doing well in the past had no correlation to success in Brenner's class. His style was like nothing we'd ever seen. Mr. Brenner would come into class each morning—Calculus class—and he'd begin by telling us some story about an engineer he knew who needed to make a bridge over a particular river. He never wrote a formula on the board; he just told you the story and you'd get more and more engrossed. The engineer was figuring this curve and that curve. And all of a sudden you'd realize you'd learned the origin of an equation. Just like that. First the story, then the epiphany, then the formula. Ten years later, I can't tell you what the formulas are, but I can tell you how they're used, how they fit into the world."

"What I go for," Brenner tells me, "what I really teach for, is the moment of 'Aha!' The moment when it all comes together. You don't get an Aha! when you're telling students the answers. It only happens when the answers come out of themselves."

Five years after Carl began teaching, he received a grant from the National Science Foundation to pursue a master's degree in mathematics. However, the year away from Alamo Heights failed to lure him into more extended study or into a career move, either out of the field or to another school. "Since that master's," says Carl with a kind of sheepish pride, "I've never spent a winter outside of this classroom in 28 years. You can see a trail worn thin from the chalkboard to the door." Carl speculates that his need for a controlled and predictable environment goes back to childhood, when school was always far from home and school friends vanished after 3 P.M., bussed to neighborhoods many miles away. At Alamo Heights High School, a stranger seems to become a part of the community after only a week or two of casual visits. Administrators hail you in the hallway, and students you passed in the lunchroom the day before acknowledge you with shy smiles. Janitors seem to have learned your name by magic. It is difficult to imagine the intimacy one must feel after 28 years in such a place.

"How do you stay fresh and enthusiastic," I ask Brenner, "teaching the same subject in the same room for such a long, long time?" He looks at me incredulously.

"Same?" he says. "There's nothing the same about it! Every year I teach different courses, or I teach the same courses differently. Every year I teach different students. It's always changing. It's never, never the same. That's why I keep writing new books. I keep thinking of new ways to do it."

"The incredible thing about Carl," says Carlyn, a colleague of his in the math department, "is this search for new ideas thing. Pretty regularly, he goes running around to everybody in the department with a copy of his latest discovery. He goes off to conferences. Most of the time he's the main speaker, but he comes back with written-up summaries — typed! — of all the workshops he's attended." She pulls from her cabinet a manila file and hands it to me. CARL'S STUFF is printed at the top. "Usually, one or two of those applies to each teacher in the department at some point or another. He just assumes we'll be interested. He assumes we'll want to experiment as much as he does."

Carlyn tells a story about testing out one of Brenner's hot-off-the-computer calculus manuscripts. "We were working out one of his problems and a student said, 'This is the hard way to do this. I can do it an easier way.' 'Go tell Mr. Brenner,' I said. And Carl changed the problem; he incorporated the boy's suggestion. Just like that."

§   §   §

It is the Friday before the Advanced Placement Calculus test, and it is raining. In Carl's A.P. Calculus class, 12 frazzled-looking seniors lounge in their chairs or sit on their desks or pace back and forth in the back of the room. Carl is drawing shapes on the blackboard: circles within circles, cones within squares. "This is Rainy Friday," he says to me when I first walk in. "Do you *know* what Rainy Friday is?" His tone reminds me of the one preteens use when exchanging adult secrets.

"Rainy Friday is no-work day," says a student in a lackadaisical voice. "Mr. Brenner draws pictures."

"What do you think *this* is?" Carl asks me, pointing to the circles within circles. "It's an Aggie firing squad," he says. The class groans at the corny joke. Aggies are Texas A & M grads. "This one's a witch fishing," Brenner continues, "and this is a bow tie caught in an elevator."

"I drew those when I was 10," sighs a blond girl with a pile of calculus notes in front of her. Carl seems to take this as a sign that the class is too nervous for humour.

"Meanwhile," he says in an old-time radio voice, "back at the calculus class."

At the far right of the blackboard, Carl has written out the class agenda for the day, as he does for every class, every day:

1. Rainy Friday
2. Everything you ever wanted to know about calculus, but were afraid to ask
3. Whatever

"Are there any last-minute confusions?" he asks. His tone has changed radically. It is fatherly, sympathetic. "How can I help you?" The rest of the period is spent in sober review, punctuated by pep talks and consolation.

§   §   §

The above exchange demonstrates something that strikes you again and again as you sit in Carl Brenner's class: his attentiveness to seismographic changes in the sensibilities of his students and to differences between one student and another. During seatwork, a tall boy in the front row cockily holds up a finished problem for Carl to check. "Dumb! Dumb! Dumb!" Carl says, giving the kid a clunk on the head. "Find your dumb mistake, you dummy." Then, 2 minutes later, he is squatting beside the desk of a delicate girl in the back, whispering to her the procedure for correcting an error. "Cal's got so much confidence," he says later, "you have to treat him roughly to get him to pay attention to details. Melissa, on the other hand, needs to be held by the hand.

"There are so many quiet triumphs and quiet tragedies that occur in these kids' lives. Incredible problems. Incredible hardships. There's a girl in my algebra class, a thalidomide baby, with no legs, only two fingers, two elbows on one arm. She walks with her crutches very, very slowly. The family is going through an ugly divorce, and the mother is an alcoholic. And with all that, this girl is incredibly mature, wise beyond her years. The other day, I walked by and stepped on her toe, her prosthesis, and I must have looked upset because she laughed and said, 'No problem! I can't feel it anyway!' Can you imagine?" Carl's whole body is into this story. He bangs his foot on the floor as if he were committing the misstep all over again. He wears a faraway gaze; he is still brooding about the encounter.

Two people besides Carl tell me another story. A young girl from a very poor family transferred to Alamo Heights from the San

Antonio Christian School. At first, intimidated by the self-confidence and affluence of her peers, she was withdrawn and isolated. But gradually she began to gain confidence and open up. One day, this girl was called out of Carl Brenner's class, sent down to the office, and told to leave the school at once. Her mother had been evicted from her apartment in the Alamo Heights district, and so she could not remain in the public school even until the end of the day. Carl's colleagues tell me that Carl, appalled at the school's rules, loaned the family the necessary $625 to pay non-resident tuition in the district until June. "She's a good girl," he says matter-of-factly. "She's good for the money. Anyway, it's these kinds of things that give the job meaning. I could be doing math as an engineer. But I wouldn't be changing lives."

When you speak to Carl, or hear what his colleagues say about him, or watch him teach, you cannot help but be struck by a certain absence of complication, the absence, perhaps, of a dark side from which his creativity might spring. Teaching for him does not seem like a substitute for other, unrealized, ambitions; nor does the affection he inspires in his students seem to fill some neurotic need for attention or love. You feel that this man is what he appears to be: a good husband, good father, regular churchgoer, basketball enthusiast, weekend scuba diver, lover of puns and wordplay and games and tricks. "He's just a great guy," says Hallie and every other colleague and former student I speak to, "warm, enthusiastic, and caring." Or as a former student teacher put it, "A person without guile, a totally ingenuous person."

§   §   §

The world of Brenner's classroom is an uncomplicated world, where only friendly competition exists and all errors can be remedied. "Tests are called 'games' in my class," he says, "and ungraded homework is called 'tests.' That way no one gets too nervous." If a student fails a test, he can copy the correct answers off the blackboard during the post-test review, and the old score will automatically be averaged in with an 80%. "That way, it is rare for someone who works with honest effort and is interested in understanding his mistakes to fail," Carl says.

One senses how difficult it is for Brenner to disappoint or punish a student, no matter how much punishment may be deserved. When an apologetic ninth grader shows up after skipping out on one of Carl's retests, the following conversation takes place.

CARL: You had an appointment, and you skipped out.
  BOY: Yeah. Yeah, I did.
CARL: What's my policy for skipping?
  BOY: You get a zero?
CARL: That's right.
  BOY: (crestfallen) That's bad. A zero is bad.
CARL: Well, if you take the test home and do it well, I'll take that into consideration.
  BOY: But can I get an A on it?
CARL: I reserve the right to change your grade, for better or worse, but probably for better.

When I ask Carl if he has a theory about discipline he says, "I *do* have a theory. You just wouldn't know it because it doesn't work. My theory is that students should be quiet while I teach." It's doubtful, though, that he means this. The success of Carl's teaching style seems contingent on a certain amount of steady noise, on questions called from the back of the room, on bad jokes eliciting groans. Every class, from first-period algebra to last-period calculus, has its own noisy games, contrived by Carl and woven into the fabric of the curriculum. One class collects quarters from Carl for errors found in the textbook. Loose change lines the upper blackboard, and students are often exclaiming over mistaken errors. In another class, Carl collects a nickel from every student, having won a bet that at least one of them would repeat "the same, dumb mistake" on a particular test question. The money, in both cases, will go for an ice-cream party at the end of the year. In general, any extended period of seriousness is punctuated by a moment of raucousness or foolishness, which Carl himself seems to enjoy as much, if not more than, the students he is entertaining.

There have been classes, Brenner admits, that have not responded to his style; classes that haven't been able to sense the subtle cues that signal: Now we are serious, now we are playful. Though he claims to be indifferent to the age and abilities of his students, Carl's greatest difficulties have tended to arise with the weakest classes. An education student at a nearby university, who spent a semester observing Carl's teaching, witnessed one such group. "These were freshmen repeaters, kids who had flunked at least once," he recalled. "They just wouldn't respond to him, or to anything. Finally Brenner said, 'Obviously, this isn't working. I'm not getting through to you. What I'd like you to do is to write down for me what you think I'm doing wrong. Tell me how I can make this class better.' And they were very candid. They said, 'Yell at us more. Don't tell corny jokes. Teach like other teachers.' He read all their suggestions, and he earnestly tried. He tried to be stern and conventional, but he just couldn't do it. He's too much the way he is."

When I ask Carl about this class, he looks vacant. "Was that a bad group?" he asks. For a moment, I think it is simply a case of faulty memory. Then I realize how little seems to perturb him for any length of time. Never, he claims, has he had any real problems with an administrator, a parent, a colleague, or a student.

§   §   §

Carl concedes that 2 out of his 28 years as a high school teacher were hard ones. The first was 1970, the year his daughter was born with a cleft palette and his father died, suddenly leaving him in charge of the family company. It was Carl's responsibility to dispose of the family assets. "I found myself traveling around the country, making deals with people, playing the godfather." At the same time, he was trying to teach his classes and, at night, tend to an infant who required almost 24-hour care. "What that year did for me," Carl remembers, "was to remind me of how much I'm really capable of doing. When I was in college (or maybe before that) I used to think, 'I can't possibly learn this. This is too difficult.' And then I'd master it and think, 'Well, that's okay, but I'll never be able to master *this*!' It was always: 'This mountain was easy, but the next one is insurmountable.' And then it isn't."

The second difficult year came when Alamo Heights High School failed to adopt his trigonometry textbook, which Carl calls the biggest blow of his career. He had deliberately removed himself from the school committee charged with making the decision, confident that the book would be chosen. When it was not, Carl says, "it blew me out of the water." No one in the department seems to remember the circumstances surrounding the book's rejection. Carl suggests, however (in words that are the closest I've ever heard him come to being negative), that the decision was very much influenced by the former chair of the department. "That teacher is no longer with us," Carl says, smiling. The book is now used by the department.

To reject Carl Brenner's textbooks is to reject a whole way of thinking about math. "My approach," he says, "connects math to life, to the way math really is used. My approach shows that math *is* life." Carl has led the way in the drive to incorporate calculators and computers into mathematics education, not just to solve problems, but to convey concepts as well. He has also brought the written word into math education, with texts that contain more narrative explanation than any others on the market. He has even succeeded in making them funny, using titles like BB Small's Rocket Problem and the hippopotamus problem.

It may be, however, that effective use of Carl Brenner's textbooks requires a predisposition toward his approach. Several years ago, an independent researcher conducted an experiment on one of Carl's textbooks and two others to see which would produce higher achievement-test scores in high school math students. Brenner's major competitor was John Saxon, who actively campaigns on behalf of his textbook throughout the Midwest and who Carl describes as an ideologue. Saxon is clearly Brenner's *bête noire*, but the experiment showed that neither text was superior to the other. Instead, student achievement correlated to the teacher's attitude towards the text, rather than to the book itself. Teachers who were sympathetic to Brenner's approach taught better with his book. Ultimately, the three textbooks came out about even, and the experiment seemed to have no impact on sales.

§   §   §

Given his renown and success, particularly his financial success, it is quite remarkable that Carl's colleagues speak so warmly and generously about him. What they say, however, shows how Carl has consciously worked on his relationships with them. He has tried to spread around the fruits of his success and study as much as he possibly can. For example, he used a large cash award received several years ago to buy the math department its own copying machine. He has also recruited colleagues to write sections of the teachers' manuals of his books, work for which they were very well paid. "Carl would love to be everybody's mentor," says a veteran member of the department. "If someone is learning the computer and is stuck, Carl will come running out of his class to help. He'll drop everything and be right there."

Indeed, if there is any trait that Carl Brenner can be criticized for, it is his seeming inability to say no. Whether it be a colleague's request for assistance, a student's plea for extra help, or an invitation to speak at a conference, Carl will attempt to find a way to "fit it in." As a result, his desk is often piled high with ungraded papers, and he has been known to forget many a department meeting.

Long-term commitments invariably lose out to immediate requests, and bureaucratic responsibilities are generally his lowest priority. Sometimes, those responsibilities fall by the wayside altogether.

Because of this quirk, it is generally agreed that Carl would make a poor department chair. When I first asked his colleagues why Carl, who has seniority in the department, had not been promoted to this position, I was confounded by their unanimous response, which was a kind of sly, conspiratorial chuckle. "Carl did apply for the position years ago," says Susan Thomas, the present chair, who beat him at the time. "I'm certain he doesn't regret losing. He knows he's no administrator."

"Look at my desk," says Carl, when I ask him about the chairmanship. "A department chair can't have a desk like that."

§   §   §

Brenner's politics are Texas politics, only slightly tempered by the skepticism found in so many public school teachers. He has been deprived or thwarted so little in his life that it may be hard for him to work up the indignation over issues that make other teachers rail. Though Carl works hard on the school's salary committee (mostly by working out the math), and though he concedes that salaries are not what they should be (in Texas they average 10–20% less than in the Northeast), he speaks without anger about the inequity, and he is not a supporter of the union. San Antonio is among the most conservative cities in the country, where the mere mention of the U-word in many schools and businesses can turn a close friend into a pariah. Carl, it seems, is a child of San Antonio and a product of its values and mores.

Carl does have a keen skepticism, however, for policy reforms that restrict the free exercise of his idiosyncratic style. In 1984, the Texas legislature passed a bill that required, among other arcane practices, the use of a rigid, quantitative instrument for teacher evaluation. It obliges the teacher under observation to open, organize, and manage his class according to a prescription. Carl says that he scored poorly on one such evaluation when his lesson for the day failed to fit into the narrow format. The incident, he says, didn't really bother him, since his renown makes his job more secure than any other in the school, but it did make him empathize with younger teachers more vulnerable to the abuses of such a practice.

Carl is equally skeptical of educational innovations such as the Coalition, a movement, led by Ted Sizer, to restructure schools from the bottom up. Recently, an Alamo Heights superintendent, newly recruited from the Northeast, attempted to foist Coalition ideas on a resistant community. "A fellow came down from Rochester," says Carl, "from a Coalition school. He told us in private that modular scheduling didn't work the way they thought it would; the 6-day period—where they have different subjects at different times over a six-day cycle—*that* didn't work. And they're going back next year to the old way, the normal way. All these new ideas, they sound good on paper, but when you get to doing them, they don't work."

Carl says that over the years he and his department have tried and abandoned a whole catalogue of supposedly new and exciting methodologies, programs, and strategies. One of these, team teaching, was briefly and unsuccessfully embraced several years ago. "Some of the teachers got together at the urging of the superintendent. But the central office made it impossible for the teachers to be successful. They never got the supplies they needed. The maintenance department didn't get their room ready until November. They put together a system that was virtually impossible to manage. . . . The department wasn't behind them." The team-teaching fiasco coincided with a school-board election. Three people were running together on a platform to stop all experimental programs. They won by a landslide.

Carl *has*, however, picked up numerous, useful classroom tricks at conferences. But these have been tried-and-true techniques proffered by real teachers. "I learned about small-group work at a conference. I learned about placing the seats in a semicircle. Using the overhead, though, that was really an overrated suggestion. It makes your classroom really hot," he says, "and it blows your papers around."

§   §   §

It is not difficult to find Carl Brenner's former students. They are everywhere in Alamo Heights, a community that rarely loses its young to larger cities, and where sons and daughters walk the same high school corridors as did their parents, grandparents, and great-grandparents. Carl's internist is an ex-student. So is the family dermatologist. So is the woman who fills his prescriptions at the pharmacy and the check-out girl at the supermarket. Carl speaks about these students with the paternalistic affection of an uncle or a godfather. "Those Hazlocker twins," he'll say, "no one thought they'd ever amount to anything. Now they're both in government. One is on the city council!" Or, "Cecelia Burk!" he says as if I know her. "She couldn't stay awake in my algebra class. . . . Now she's been elected tax assessor in Travis County." Carl's memory for such details is extraordinary.

And so is the memory of Brenner's former students for him. Every ex-student I encountered, whether at dinner parties, the symphony, or the park, leapt at the opportunity to tell a story. One recalled how Brenner "saved my brother from becoming a good-for-nothing" and another how he "attended every single one of my basketball games." Yet another remarked on how Brenner's own "boyishness and shyness made it feel all right for us to be awkward." "I can't think of anyone I had more respect for in high school," said one 10-year alumna. "When we had a substitute," she said to illustrate, "I would never dream of acting out. And not because we were afraid of getting in trouble, but out of just not wanting to disappoint him. Not that he had any terrible power over me," she says, "but the respect, the respect was so great. It would be like letting down my own father."

§   §   §

On the first day of the last week of classes, two days before the final exam, Carl's fourth-period algebra students squirm in their seats. Carl is reviewing the long division of polynomials, making his way through a number of sample problems on the board, trying to extract input from a sullen, weary class. "Why do we have to do this?" calls out a girl with an exaggerated pout. "I'm going to be an actress," she says, "I'm never going to use this in my life."

"You never know," says Carl. "You never know how you can use math. There was a student once, a student like you, who graduated and went to Austin and became a choreographer. She was good in math, interested in math. And she decided to base a dance on the Fibonacci sequence: 1, 1, 2, 3, 5, 8, 13. She knew from math that those numbers are mystical, that they appear in nature with strange regularity: in the rings of a pineapple or on a pine cone. And because she knew math, this choreographer could make fascinating patterns based on the sequence. . . . It was a wonderful dance."

The class sits, transfixed, during this story. Then all turn silently back to their long division.

§   §   §

    That evening, I stand with a kitchen knife poised above a newly purchased pineapple. Counting the rings—eight in one direction, 13 in the other—I observe the way they intersect to form a delicate network of squares along the prickly walls of the fruit. "Math is the foundation of everything," says Carl. "Math is life." And suddenly (Aha!) I understand what he means by this, and how remarkable it is that he has made me see it!

3 Andy Galligani

In the main office of West Morris Central High, Andy Galligani's school in Long Valley, New Jersey, the day is about to begin. It is 7:25 on a late-fall morning, close enough to Thanksgiving for the first signs of exhaustion to be visible on the faces of arriving teachers. The office, like the halls and facade of this sprawling brick building, is immaculate, generously proportioned, and attractively adorned. It is not the cramped, stained, paper-laden office of an urban school. The students who enter and leave, carrying brightly colored book bags and satchels decorated with the school emblem, seem perfectly suited to their surroundings. Their faces are open, scrubbed, and uniformly Caucasian. Their clothes are simple and conservative, more J.C. Penney than Fiorucci. One girl, in a tartan-plaid skirt and lace-up boots, shifts back and forth uneasily before the main desk. "What is it, young lady?" asks the burly vice principal who is sorting through file cards.

"I was absent yesterday. I brought a note, sir," says the girl.

"Is there a rest room nearby?" I ask the boy sitting next to me, who is bent over his algebra book, studying intensely.

"Yes, indeed, ma'am. Down the hall, ma'am." As a veteran urbanite, new to such courtesies, my first impulse is to suspect him of sending me in the wrong direction.

Andy arrives to fetch me at 7:30. He is a man who is always punctual, if not early, a trait rooted in his childhood spent on a farm. "So you found the damned place," he snaps, shaking my hand hard. The gruff voice and brashness stand in powerful contrast to the genteel cheerfulness of all that preceded his entrance. No one that I was to meet in the whole school would act or talk remotely like this stern, barrel-chested man limping across the office in a flannel shirt and woodsman's jacket.

§   § -   §

This morning, in senior honors English, Andy is teaching "The Road Not Taken," by Robert Frost. Having moved the class carefully through the first three stanzas of the poem, Andy is now letting them grapple with the last five lines. Several students in the class feel that the final stanza is "too corny," that it "sounds like something out of the Farmer's Almanac." Others feel this stanza is the one that makes the poem great.

"Read the lines out loud," says Andy, interrupting the rising commotion. "Read them in the way you think they're supposed to be read."

A girl in the first row volunteers, then reads the stanza with exaggerated theatricality:

> I shall be telling this with a sigh
> Somewhere ages and ages hence:
> Two roads converged in a wood, and I—
> I took the one less travelled by,
> And that has made all the difference.
>
> (Robert Frost, "The Road Not Taken")

"I think the way you read the lines is interesting," Andy says after a brief silence. "What was Eleanor trying to show us by the way she read the lines?"

"That this is something really earthshaking that's happened?"

"Is it?" asks Andy, "Is it earthshaking that he takes one road and not another? Do you really think it changed the course of his life—as the poem implies?"

Yeses and no's float up from various corners of the room.

"Simon," Andy says to a red-headed boy beside him, "you said yes. Explain what you mean."

"Well, you've said before that we define ourselves by the choices we make. Every single choice influences your fate. This guy's decided to take the less travelled road. . . . "

"What does that mean, the 'less travelled road?'" asks Andy.

"The less popular road; like to be a poet and not a stockbroker" says the red-headed boy. "To be a teacher and not a lawyer." The class laughs.

"Good!" says Andy. "So the poet is saying that our choices are very important; they define who we are . . . But is there anything else going on here? Look carefully at the wording. Remember that for a poet, every word is very important. What do you make of the phrase, 'ages and ages hence'?"

Slowly Andy begins to pull a second, contradictory meaning from the lines. The poet, he shows, is actually making fun of himself. He is ridiculing his own impulse to myth-make — to elevate his life to heroic proportions.

"So the road he takes," says a girl in a frustrated voice, "*does* it make a difference or *doesn't* it?"

"Exactly," says Andy. "That's exactly the question the poet wants you to ask." And he turns to the next poem.

§   §   §

When people talk about Andy-the-teacher or Andy-the-teacher-trainer, they tend to liken him to an assortment of great or infamous men, men whose accomplishments or personalities have made them larger than life. He has been compared to Emerson, John Dewey, and Napoleon. But when Andy talks about his childhood, the comparison that seems most apt is the one made by a former student who has maintained close ties with him over the years. "Andy," he says, "is a Lincoln. A self-made man. A wood-splitting scholar who worked his way up from poverty. In part, it's his childhood that makes him the remarkable teacher he is."

Indeed, to hear the story of Andy's childhood is to have an even greater respect for his later achievements. Born in 1926, the youngest child in an impoverished family of eight, Andy began life with the double handicap of poverty and disease. An attack of polio in infancy left him severely crippled in one leg, and vulnerable to illness. "I can remember getting sick all the time," he says, "and not only me, but my brothers and sisters too. Because we were so hungry. And if we ate food, we ate it so fast we got sick again."

Even the barest necessities, such as clothes and clean water, were often inadequate. Andy speaks of winter mornings when his sisters were forced to go off to school without underwear. He remembers his own mortification when, after being warned several times by a teacher about his poor hygiene, he was taken to a back room and scrubbed clean in front of several classmates. "I felt clean for the first time in I don't know how long. It was a good feeling, but I was humiliated in front of the other kids."

Perhaps the greatest deprivation of all was the absence of a positive father figure. "My father was a waiter," he explains, "in Washington, New York, Atlantic City. He was away from home most of the time. When he did get back, for a week or so every few months, he'd use those days to discipline us." Andy speaks of his father as if he were a vague phantom, neither loved nor hated, who was nonetheless capable of deeply hurting his son. "My father was a person with a sense that everything should be right. One time, for example, he said that if I really wanted to, I didn't have to walk the way I was walking—like a cripple. If I really tried, he said, I could walk straight. And he would tell me to bend my ankle, which was impossible because it was fused."

As Andy relates these painful, almost Dickensian tales of suffering, his voice betrays no shred of judgment or emotion. Nor does he seem to have elevated his childhood memories to the status of myth. His accounts of his mother's mental illness and his brother's death are told in the same matter-of-fact tone that he uses to describe his schooling, his job search, or his marriage.

With no father to turn to for guidance and support, Andy found his first mentor in the father of a friend. It was at this neighbor's farm that he first came to relish what he calls recreational reading. "Over at the neighbors," he recalls, "they had *Reader's Digest* and *Harper's*, and a few others like *Life*. I used to read them avidly, and pick up vocabulary from them. *Reader's Digest* used to have vocabulary tests, and I was good at taking them. This friend's father, he'd encourage me with little remarks like, 'You've got a good head, Andy,' or 'Gee, you're pretty intelligent.' It really sunk in, because I'd never heard praise from an adult."

Andy first experienced the politics of education, which he would come to loathe later in life, when he was still in grammar school. "I was always good in the classroom," he says, "in the top reading groups, the top math groups. But because I was from the other side of the tracks—not the son of someone in the fire department or the police department or on the board of education—the teachers looked down on me. I was pretty much on my own as far as motivation goes."

Nor did that change when it came time for Andy to go to college. By then, his older brothers were already quite successful financially. But none of them was willing to part with a nickel. Clearly, generosity and sacrifice were not part of the family credo. "When someone in my family got out and did for himself, that was it," Andy says. "It was every man for himself. Nobody was going to help anybody else out in any measurable way. That was instilled in us from the time food was first put on the table. Whoever got it was the one who grabbed it first. It's a hard lesson to unlearn."

§   §   §

Andy entered Rutgers University on a full scholarship. His initial intention was to become a minister, because he knew he liked "to read and to talk to people." A minister in his church, a friendly and intelligent man, applauded his decision and suggested he join the Future Ministers Club. "As soon as I joined that group, it only took me a month to be disgusted with it," Andy recalls. "They were no more interested in the spiritual life than the man in the moon. They could only talk about fraternities and all kinds of things that would bring them higher social rank. I might as well have gone into business management and heard the same kind of talk.

"But in the meantime, I had some very good friends studying literature, and they'd have very interesting bull sessions about what they were learning, . . . and I got interested in it. There was one fellow in these sessions — he was 32 and I was maybe 18 or 19 — he said to me, 'Andy, the best thing you can do if you want to get to the minds of people is be a teacher. If you're going to be a preacher standing in the pulpit, you're going to be talking to people in their 50s or 60s, or near death who just want a little safety before they die. The young people aren't even going to hear you, and what they do hear they're not going to use anyway. But young people have formative minds. . . . ' And I said to myself, 'Of course! If I have this thing for trying to get people to get some quality out of their lives, the best place to start is with young people. And what better vehicle than English or English literature?' "

Andy's switch to English literature was satisfying, but finding a job after graduation was not easy. In 1949, high school jobs were scarce, and every institution that advertised an opening was flooded with applications. Andy had signed up with a placement service at Temple University, where he was taking several graduate courses in education, and he remembers a string of unsuccessful interviews in the summer and fall of that year. "I have to think that because I limp when I walk, that was against me," he says in his characteristically matter-of-fact way. "I wasn't resentful, because I expected it. If two people walked in, and one walked normally and one didn't the guy who walked normally was ahead of me."

Then a friend advised him to try elementary school teaching, where positions were available. After several years in an elementary classroom, he was told, he could move easily into a job as principal or superintendent. But Andy recognized that he did not have the right temperament, and chose to persist with his original plan. In February, he gritted his teeth and returned to the schools that had rejected him the previous year. "What did I do wrong?" he asked. "How could I have interviewed better? What does the guy you hired have that I don't have?" Quite to his own surprise, his moxie paid off. A midyear opening at one of the schools needed to be filled at once, and Andy got the job.

§   §   §

Andy's work at Clayton High School in Abington Township, New Jersey, was not his first experience with teaching. The summer after college, he had enrolled in a student teaching program in which he worked with four students in each class. There, according to Andy, his skill in the use of a stapler and how to erase the blackboard was assessed. "I had some gal, some supervisor, who was deeply concerned with whether I could use a hole punch. She gave me a C in the course . . . though she was gracious enough to put down that I knew the material well; that I got along with the kids. I just couldn't do practical things. I remember I was giving the kids a final exam, and during the exam she came in and said the kids should have all their papers stapled together. I said, 'I don't want to bother them right now, they're taking an exam,' and that if every-thing has to be stapled together, I would take care of it after the exam. And she said, 'No, you should do it now.' She just grabbed the stapler and went around to the kids, and stapled. It sounds so trivial, but this girl made it a big comment about my ability to teach."

Andy has unmitigated scorn not only for the priorities of this supervising teacher, but for all the education courses he has taken in his career as well, starting in college. He articulates his complaint in virtually every conversation he has about education. Language is abused by educators, he says. Shop talk has become double-talk. Form has replaced substance. "When I started to get the flavor of what it was like to be in education courses, somehow my English training made me look at that kind of language and that kind of superficial talk as disgusting. It would be like a person who's learned to appreciate Milton trying to get satisfaction out of reading *Little Red Riding Hood*.

"I realized it first when I was at Rutgers. The dean allowed me to carry something like 24 credits each semester so I could get the teaching and methods courses. He knew, I guess, how little substance there was in those courses. The textbooks! They were so long-winded and didn't say a damn thing. And I got so frustrated with having to sit and wade through something that meant nothing. . . . Like, 'If the climate is appropriate, then education will take place with effectiveness to the degree that all is well.' You go around in these circles again and again. People seem to thrive on it . . . except the teachers in the classroom, all of whom made fun of it. They made fun of it in those days, and they make fun of it today, and the only time they don't is when they're getting into administration. Then all of a sudden, it's not to be made fun of anymore."

Despite his ferocious antipathy to educational jargon, Andy persisted with the courses and completed his master's degree. He knew it was the ticket not only to a higher salary, but also to a more affluent school. At Clayton, his salary was only $2,200 a year, and he was responsible for 146 students, two drama productions, and the yearbook.

By April of his first year, Andy was forced to take a part-time job in the auto-sales department at Sears Roebuck. "I worked every Friday night and all day Saturday," Andy remembers, "and I could pick up $15–$18 dollars, which in 1950 was a lot of money. Then one day, early in the summer, one of the bigshots came down to the floor and spoke to me very, very nicely. I wasn't used to this kind of treatment—being in education, I was used to being battered around. But this fellow treated me as though I was the pivotal person needed by Sears Roebuck. He asked me what my salary was. I told him the next year's salary, because I was embarrassed to tell him my present one, and he looked at me and said, 'I see' in a very cultivated way. He said to me, 'Mr. Galligani, we're very pleased with your work here. Extraordinarily pleased.' And I had never heard that in teaching. Everybody was always criticizing. Nobody ever said, 'You're working hard. You're doing well.' And he said, 'If you could consider it, we'd like to have you work full-time here.' And he said, 'I can personally guarantee you that you would make at the very minimum twice the salary you're making now. There's a chance you could make much more than that.' Then he told me about their savings programs and a program where they match your purchase of Sears stock. . . . So I swallowed hard, because I have to admit I like money and I'm a greedy person. But I was still in the throes of my need to talk to people and interest them in ideas. I was very impressed with what college had done for me, and I wanted to see if I could spread it around a little. By the time the week was over, I had turned him down."

§   §   §

Ironically, Andy's decision to stay in teaching resulted not in his return to the classroom, but in a switch to the position of vice principal, and enrollment in yet another education program at Rutgers. By his second year at Clayton, Andy's reputation as a superb teacher and unwavering disciplinarian had spread north. Without even observing his teaching, Morris Hills — a wealthier district — hired Andy as a three-quarter–time administrator, for the royal sum of $3,500 a year. One of the stipulations of his appointment was that he complete the graduate courses needed to obtain a principal's certificate.

Once again, Andy found himself profoundly at odds with the teacher of one of his education courses. "This fellow Paxton gave out to students a paper and talked about it as one of the 'best pieces of educational research I've ever read.' He told us to read and critique the paper. So I read it, and it was all this wordy, verbose, noncommunicative style of writing and I don't know how he could have said it was a good piece of research, because I didn't see any research involved in it. I'd read Spinoza, Descartes, Hume, and I'd gotten an A in Philosophy at Rutgers, but by the time I'd read this paper, I was convinced I'd read nothing. Just meaningless words. So that's what I wrote him, using quotes to demonstrate my point. I said, 'The essence of this piece seems to be one of those typical clichés: The climate of the high school is dependent on the climate established by the superintendent. It's like saying a person feels comfortable depending on the kind of weather that suits him.' He gave me a C-D in the course, which meant that if I were willing to rewrite my critique, he would change it to B. Being the kind of guy I was, I refused to do it, of course. I refused to cater to the hypocrisy. These guys talk about democracy in education and getting everybody's input, but they were the most God awful tyrants in the classroom when it came to what you could or couldn't say. As long as you echoed their line, you were an A student. It just ran against my grain."

Andy has a long-standing dissatisfaction with administrators that seems to date from his brief experience as a vice principal. Around his fellow administrators, he felt the same way he did around the ministry students. Both, he says, preferred talking to doing. "Education is bifurcated into two groups," Andy observes, "those who make their profession talking about teaching, and those who teach. And when the ones in the second group — the teachers —

make their way into the first group — the administrators — they forget everything they knew. They sit around and talk all day about all the wonderful things that should happen in the classroom, all the great things and neat ideas. It's a fine way to make a living if you don't give a damn about anything. When real teachers talk about the reality of teaching it bores people. Because like any other profession, a lot of it is routine, trivial. But you have to do it. You need to have books, pencils; kids need to be sitting still. While the administrators see it all like the Laputans in *Gulliver's Travels*. They sail above everything that's real and talk in long, complicated sentences, and then they float away thinking they've made a contribution."

But when Andy petitioned to return to the classroom full-time, he ran into unforeseen difficulties. The superintendent who had promoted him, who, in effect, had taken Andy under his wing, perceived the request as a betrayal. Months passed, and the superintendent failed to respond. When August came without a word about his teaching position, Andy accepted a job at another school.

§   §   §

Hanover Park High School was in the process of being reorganized along new, progressive lines. The superintendent had introduced new programs, a new curriculum, and a new physical plant. The experiment was in its second year when Andy arrived to help salvage it. "They'd decided everything would be different — the environment, the discipline — but the kids practically drove the teachers out of the school, out of the community! I found this out after I got there. They were looking for people who could keep an iron rein on the students. They gave me the classes that were considered unteachable, and paid me the same salary I was getting at Morris Hills to be an administrator. Money was not a problem for them. Chaos was."

It does not require a lot of imagination to envision Andy Galligani taming even the fiercest collection of delinquents. Even though he is deaf in one ear and is currently recovering from the flu, it is clear that no student in his morning section of English 9 is a match for him. "This was a sort of wild group the first week or two," he says. "It took me a little while to teach them what's what."

"What's what" seems to be communicated through a strategy that might best be described as playful intimidation. "Greg!" he snaps at a boy who is lingering near the back of the room after the bell has sounded. "Do you know where your seat is?" Before the offender can respond, Andy is at him. "I know it's hard for you to remember now — a strain on your intelligence. But think how easy it will be to find it in 3 months!" Andy then turns to the rest, "I'm really angry with this class. Really, really angry. I told the substitute yesterday what a horrible, stupid bunch you were. And what happens? You act good and intelligent with her. You've made me into a liar, and I'm really mad."

Whether or not this sarcasm registers with all the students is unclear. But certainly the quips have the effect of silencing them, of keeping them, as Andy says, "in a constant state of doubt and unease, the ideal condition for learning.

"When it comes to discipline," he says, "what I tell new teachers is: 'You have to learn how to be a bitch. Even if it means you have to go home and practice in front of the mirror. Because if you know *how* to be a bitch, you rarely have to *be* a bitch in the classroom. But if you don't know how to be a bitch, watch out. The kids will turn you into a cynical person, and you'll leave the profession thinking kids are the worst thing in the world.'"

§   §   §

Andy spent only one year at Hanover Park, but it was not the discipline problem that ultimately drove him away. It was the philosophy. He quickly found in the doctrine of progressivism all that he most loathed in education: the hollow rhetoric, the euphemisms, the laxity disguised as rigor. Innovative administrators at Hanover enforced a so-called new vocabulary of progressivism that went deeply against the grain of Andy's commonsensible approach. "We were not allowed to talk about 'English,' for example; we were only allowed to talk about 'language arts.' You did not mention 'grammar.' You could say 'language structure,' but you couldn't say 'grammar.'

"The fellow who ran the English Department was a graduate of Harvard, but he didn't know which end was up, and when I got into that department and said, 'What am I supposed to teach?', he said, 'If you just go into the closet and find something you're familiar with, just get that and teach it.' I said, 'Are there any grammar books?' And he said, 'Sir, we teach language structure here,' and he drew a circle on the board with lots of spokes in it. By the time he got finished with his demonstration, he had a system so complicated that even if I had learned it, it wouldn't have been a good way to teach grammar because the system itself would have been harder to learn than the grammar!"

Andy claims that he could have stayed at Hanover Park and done what he wanted to do in the classroom while pretending to toe the party line. "It was the easiest job I ever had," he says, "because nobody supervised. I was never once observed. And the chairman of the department was so disorganized that really you could do anything you wanted. They had a reading teacher there, for instance, who was great for demonstrating the latest clothing styles to kids, playing them rock-and-roll, and having them jump around the room. She didn't teach them much reading, but of course she was heralded as a great teacher, and went on to become a reading instructor at Rutgers. . . . That's what they went for—'getting with it with the kids' and making sure it's 'child-centered.' All these phrases that made those of us who were trying to *teach* kids feel as though we hated kids, didn't give a damn, or understand that kids were sensitive. That progressive approach is calculated to make you feel guilty. But you know, the kids actually resented the adults for trying to enter their world. Kids *want* to be led into the adult world. But the adults were saying, 'We'll become like them, and then they'll like us.' Of course, the kids didn't protest openly, because it meant they were getting much less work. But inwardly, they resented it, the way a person might resent your giving him money all the time. . . .

"There were other teachers at Hanover who did sense it as I did. One Spanish teacher named Esposito kept up his standards, too. He was a strict teacher, and they used to bitch and moan about it, but you could see in the classroom that they relied on him, because if they were as angry as they claimed to be you would have seen it in their actions. But Esposito's classes were deferential towards him. If he dropped a piece of paper or a book, they'd rush to pick it up. These are the little clues that kids give out to show they respect you. It's a body language more than a spoken language."

§   §   §

When asked to summarize his educational philosophy, Andy says, "I am teaching people who know absolutely nothing about my subject, so it's up to me to say, 'Here is what you should learn in order to become more educated. If you use these disciplines I'm imparting to you, your mind will be better. If you don't, it won't.' Education is the transfer of information as well as the technique of how to use it. A good teacher teaches not only what a noun is, but how a noun functions in a sentence. Now, in order to teach a kid what a noun is, I have to have him memorize certain things about grammar. It's a rote operation having nothing to do with his enlightenment. . . . In other words, first you learn the tools for perception — an arduous and dull process. Then the capacity to reason begins. Then everything opens up. But I bet that most of the things you do when you start thinking go back to something that's internally structured in your head through the process of rote recitation. There's a very important place in education for that. I know from experience that to teach a kid to write, he has to go through a process of memorization, learning an alphabet of forms and structures. There's no shortcut. No easy route. Now, a progressive educator would say I'm killing their creativity, stifling their minds. What I'm doing is teaching them discipline, and it's from discipline that creativity comes."

§   §   §

This traditional philosophy of education is the one that Andy brought with him to the newly opened school to which he came after Hanover Park — West Morris Central — where he has remained for the past 27 years. There, Andy found the position for which he feels he is best suited, that of English Department chair. In this role, he has been able to articulate and refine his ideas about teaching. He has also been able to pass those ideas on to other educators.

Some of Andy's most passionate followers are teachers within the department whom he has trained. Many of them speak about him in such hyperbolic terms, it seems at first that they have been coached. But their anecdotes soon make it clear that their debt to Andy is profound and sincere. "Andy Galligani completely changed my life," one 14-year veteran of the department confided. "When I was starting out, he spent hours and hours with me after school, sometimes into the evening. He taught me a whole new way to look at literature. He taught me how *kids* perceive literature . . . how to relate the literature to their lives. He would role-play for me how to discipline a class. 'Never be confrontational,' he would say. 'Never make it into an enemy thing. Never say: "You don't want to learn." Say: "I can't teach you if you're not paying attention."' He has a remarkable perception about the way kids are. And his advice is concrete, practical."

Ann, a new teacher who recently made the leap from advertising into education, remembers the first time she had to teach *Macbeth*. "I panicked. I told Andy, 'I can't teach this stuff; I can barely understand it myself.' I was trying to cram all this criticism into my head. And Andy said, 'Figure out what you *do* understand in the play and teach that. Don't try and pretend you know more than you do.'"

When I ask Andy to instruct me as if I were a new recruit, he launches into his "guide to teacher training:" "Here are the books you are to teach," he says. "None of this choosing your own books. And here is the text you're going to use to teach the grammar, because you *are* going to teach grammar. And here is the vocabulary you're going to use when you teach it. Now the vocabulary may be different from what you're used to, but it shouldn't be different from the concepts you know. I want the kids to hear the same vocabulary from all my English teachers. I don't want them to hear 'noun' from one and 'nominative indicator' from another. Kids have a hard enough time, so the vocabulary should be pretty much standardized. . . . If that conflicts with your religion, you'd better let me know so we can discuss it. Now, when it comes to literature, I want you to teach *defensively*. You've read this book; maybe you don't know what you want the kids to do with it. Well, I have a great faith in reading; I have a great faith in saying to the kids, 'I've assigned you this story. Now prove to me that you've read it.' Teach on a content level. What is this story about? Who are the characters? Then, once you continue to teach the works, you begin to find ideas in them. As you discover these ideas, incorporate them into your teaching. But do it gradually, and make sure they are *your* ideas. . . .

"I believe in learning by watching other teachers," Andy continues. "I always tell new teachers to use their department assignment time to visit the classrooms of successful colleagues. 'Just watch them,' I say. 'If you want to feel inadequate, fine. But I want you to see what happens in a good classroom so we can talk about something concrete.' After the observation, I can say, 'Did you notice the way the teacher started his class? He started immediately. He knew immediately what he wanted to do in the first 10 seconds. If he didn't, the kids would get the idea they could get away with things. . . . Kids love to bait the teacher. A class is a vicious animal—it likes to see suffering. And you have to short-circuit that.'"

§   §   §

Listening to Andy, it is not difficult to understand why he has made a number of powerful enemies in the course of his career. According to many who have worked with him for years, it is his methods and uncompromising standards that have angered parents, alienated administrators, and caused major upheavals at the board of education. "Usually he's accused of rigidity and insensitivity," says Sam, a longtime friend and advocate. "Periodically, whenever grade-point averages fall below a certain point, they try to get on his case. They've even tried hounding him out at various times. But it never works. He has too many supporters, too many people who know real value when they see it."

Andy invariably responds to criticism by attacking his attackers with redoubled force. He is a fighter by nature; a man who his friends say has never been able to compromise. "Over the years," says a colleague, "when he's come in conflict with the board over things like watering down the curriculum or accepting insubstantial programs, he hasn't budged an inch."

Andy has also provoked criticism within his own department. Though he has a large number of ardent followers, individuals who testify to his brilliance and his vision, others feel that he is not as tolerant of diversity as he should be, especially given his own impatience with educational ideologues. One 10-year department veteran, for instance, shook her head sadly when asked about her relationship with Andy. "He took me under his wing and gave me an interesting, fruitful way of looking at literature. But he left me no room to grow. 'This is the way to do it,' he said. Once he told me, and I'll never forget it, that my ideas were nebulous non-ideas. It was devastating to me. . . . He has all these disciples, but sometimes a disciple needs to break away."

One of Andy's earliest disciples is his wife, Cindy. An attractive, highly articulate woman 10 years younger than her husband, Cindy has become a strong force in her own right at West Morris High. Quietly, she has managed to have a feminist perspective incorporated into the English curriculum, and as a result, books by Toni Morrison and Doris Lessing are now being taught.

A delicate balance characterizes the relationship between Andy and Cindy Galligani, a balance that seems to have been achieved through hard-won compromises. On one side there is Andy's Italian machismo, and on the other, Cindy's feminist values. At home, however, the family roles are conventionally divided. Cindy has always, according to Andy, assumed most of the household burden. He speaks of her responsibility for getting meals on the table and caring for the kids, in addition to teaching, as if this were the way it had to be. He talks about his own chores—chopping wood, managing the family finances, and caring for the exterior of the house—in the same way. Cindy often teases Andy about his antediluvian views regarding their domestic situation, but she accepts it none-the-less. "These were patterns set long before women started questioning their roles," she says. And now, with her children grown and out of the house, these issues no longer seem of great importance.

The house itself, a hilltop split level, is a source of great pride to Andy, and seems to be almost an extension of the man himself. He designed it and helped build it, and so, it is a product of both his imagination and labor. When Andy speaks of retiring and spending "more time with the house," it is as if the house were an alter ego whose leaking roof or flooded basement represented a kind of argument between friends.

§   §   §

"Ask Andy to talk to you about language," a former student tells me over the phone. "That's the key to his genius."

"It's true, it's almost an obsession of mine," says Andy, when I tell him what the student said. "The lesson I try to press home again and again is that the abuse of language causes all the tragedy and heartbreak in the world. When I teach, I say to the students, 'My gosh, look at these characters in literature and watch what they say. Don't judge them and don't make fun of them; don't call them names. Just watch what happens. The most well-intentioned individual, the person who is the kindest, the most generous, and outgoing individual in the world gets into the most god-awful dramatic tragedies, not because of any character flaw or any inner meanness, but because he doesn't understand what he's doing with words.'

"King Lear couldn't be a better case in point. Look at Lear with his three daughters. He wants to do well by his three daughters, but first he wants to know that they love him. Now, his test for love is the words they use. The two who don't love him are free to manufacture all kinds of words, but the one who really does love him has a sense of that reality, and knows that the words are inadequate to express the love she has for him. Not only that, but she knows enough about love to know that if you can love one person, you can love more than one. She can't very well explain that to her father, although she does try in a haphazard sort of way. She says, 'I'm married to this man. I love him. But I also love you.' But when Lear hears that, to him 'love' means 'exclusion'—you love me to the exclusion of anybody else . . . which is not a definition of love, certainly not in the Christian sense of the word. Now here's a man who is the spiritual leader of a Christian nation, who doesn't even understand what they've been talking about in church, in the Bible. For Lear, love and words are the same thing. And that's what gets him in trouble.

"I think that's what people don't see in literature, that words are simply sounds that don't necessarily convey right meaning. The word is *not* the thing. . . . It's very plain that people are, as the Greeks say, 'doomed to tragedy,' because every time a man uses a word, he thinks he's right because he's used the right word."

§   §   §

It is a similar lesson about language that Andy is trying to convey to his ninth-grade class on a particularly wintry morning in early December. The text is *To Kill a Mockingbird*, and judging from the rumblings that preceded the class, it is receiving only mixed reviews. The major complaint, it seems, is that the main character, Atticus, doesn't "do" anything. "You said Atticus was the hero of the book," says a small, blond girl in the front row. "But so far all he's done is shoot a mad dog."

"If you were the readers I'd like you to be, you'd see already that there's more to Atticus than meets the eye, that he is indeed a hero," Andy says gruffly.

"Is it because he's patient of others?" offers the same girl.

"Patient? What does that word *patient* mean? A hunter can be patient when he's stalking his prey. Is that what you mean?"

"Tolerant, kind," adds another girl, defensively. "Like how the town is against blacks, and he defends them."

"But isn't that stupid of him?" says Andy. "Isn't he crazy to take that kind of risk—a man with a family?"

The class is quiet, ruminating. It is clear that Andy's method of calling into question every word or phrase, his insistence on precision, is painful for some of the students. There is much frustrated shrugging and sighing.

In the end, though, a quiet boy with a furrowed brow suddenly pulls together all the pieces Andy has left dangling. "I guess we can never exactly know what a hero is," he says carefully, watching Andy closely as he speaks. "But in this book, it seems like Atticus is a hero because he's got the courage to stand up for what he believes, even if it does mean personal risk."

There is a moment of silence, and then the class breaks into applause. "Yes," says Andy, smiling one of his rare smiles. "Very good. That's what a hero is. That's the thing most kids don't understand."

§   §   §

When I ask Andy whether, from his present vantage point, he would again choose teaching as a career if he had to start all over, he is silent for awhile. "If you asked me that 10 years ago," he says finally, "I would have said, 'Yes! Yes! Without a doubt!' Maybe it's because I'm about to retire, maybe I'm just tired, . . . but right now I'd have to say, 'I'm not sure.' Teaching today isn't what it used to be."

The major, troubling change that Andy sees in education today is the degree to which the profession has become an extension of community politics. "Politics have corrupted the classroom," he says. "The people on the board, the ones who force policy in the classroom, are invariably people with kids in the school. They want their kids to do well, so they push to lower the standards for everybody.

"I used to like to teach the honors classes. But today the honors classes are not what they once were — because of politics. We established, in the beginning, four levels of English, . . . because kids perform at different levels. But by the time this translates to the public, it reads as 'The basic English course is for the scum bags, and the honors classes are for the elite.' And, of course, I want my kid to be elite. So you end up getting kids in the honors classes who don't belong there, and the kids in the basic classes are only there because they want to hold a full-time job while going to school. It has nothing to do with ability anymore."

Andy sees other practical deterrents to teaching as well, ones that have to do with changes in the culture at large. "I think teenagers now belong to a wholly separate culture. I think the old Pied Piper that Browning wrote about, he's around more than I ever dreamed. So that when kids are born, they are almost immediately taken away from you by the radio, by the media, by television. Parents don't have the same control over their children that they once did, even in the 60s and 70s. Now they're frightened of their children. So when their kids complain about this or that in the school, anything that dissatisfies them, the parents get all hyper because they want to prove to their kids that they're on their side. This fear comes out in many ways: 'My kid needs support.' 'My kid shouldn't be given a hard time.' 'Things should be easy for my child.' And teachers have caught on to this to the point where there are teachers who will give nothing below a B. Such teachers are never in controversial situations. You may hear the complaint that schools inflate grades; schools don't teach anything. . . . But God forbid you try to do anything concrete about it. This whole idea of being child-centered is for the birds. You can't teach Browning or Milton or calculus or physics if you're worried about being child-centered."

Given such sentiments, it is no surprise that Andy sees both special education and mainstreaming as misguided enterprises, a drain on school resources. Of mainstreaming he says, pointing to his lame foot, "It's like putting *me* in a regular physical education class. We have these handicapped kids, these troubled kids in the classes with the regular students, and all it does is heighten their awareness of their own deficiencies. What's more, it breeds resentment from kids, resentment from faculty. Special ed teachers have drastically limited enrollments in their classes, . . . while regular teachers slog along with up to 30. And many of the regular kids have lots of problems too. Then there are these child study teams . . . people who know no more than me or you about these kids, but who are deemed experts because they've learned some jargon.

"I don't believe in psychologists or psychiatrists; they come with a battery of clichés. Once I was having trouble with a kid in my class. He was being rude and obnoxious, and the school psychologist said, 'Well, we have this student down as being socially maladjusted.' 'Socially maladjusted? What do you mean by socially maladjusted?' I said. 'Wasn't Einstein socially maladjusted?' And the psychologist was just baffled. She had nothing to say."

§   §   §

It is a Saturday evening in late May. From the middle of the smoky, densely packed room at the Lamplight Inn, I can hear Andy laughing. It is the first time, I realize, that I have ever heard him do so. This is Andy's retirement dinner. Having begun 35 years ago in midyear at Clayton, Andy is departing midyear from West

Morris Central, with Cindy newly instated as department chair. Surrounding him now, like the figures at the end of Fellini's $8\frac{1}{2}$, are all the allies and detractors — the villains and clowns — that Andy has described to me over the course of our talks, a whole career in a single room.

"Do you think he's tipsy?" I ask one of Andy's longtime friends, as we observe him laughing through a break in the crowd.

"Andy never drinks," my companion says. "He must be very, very happy. He's come to the end of a long love-hate relationship."

After dinner, after the praise and the tearful recollections, Andy draws me over to his side. "This must be damn dull for you," he says.

"Oh, no!" I say. "This is a revelation to me. And besides, now I can ask you how you feel about leaving."

"For the most part, I feel greatly relieved," he says.

"And the other part?"

"I really wanted to change the world." He smiles. "And even though I came to know I couldn't do it, I never gave up thinking that I could. That's the stubbornness in me."

4   Lily Chin

Brackenridge High School in San Antonio, Texas, is located just south of the center of town, where tourists stroll along the riverbanks or ride barges past the facades of quaint, Mexican-style hotels and restaurants. A river-front room at the new Marriott Hotel rents for over $200 a night, and a small silver bracelet, which might sell for $30 across the Mexican border, goes for an easy $300 in the fashionable shops of River Center Mall.

Though it is only 5 minutes away, the world of Brackenridge High School is very far away from all of this. Just beyond the sports arena and the symphony hall, the streets become narrow and poorly paved. Tall hotels are replaced by single-level garages, open markets, and boarded-up billiard parlors. Across from the school is a sprawling, shabby subdivision, The Courts, where each small house has a metal fence and rusty window grilles.

The high school itself has the clean, severe lines of schools built in the early 1970s, when designs reflected the prevailing notion of the school-as-prison. It is a huge, windowless building that stretches for almost a city block and is unlandscaped outside. Inside, one enters to find a giant mall area, which functions as lunchroom, auditorium, and social center. The administration offices front this mall to the left, receding into dozens of tiny cubicles behind the plate-glass window of the main office.

When I arrive on a late-spring morning, first period has already begun. There are no students around, except for a silent line of young people who lean against the wall outside a room marked CLINIC. They are mostly girls, in tight capri pants and bangs moussed straight up. One boy, in a football jersey, rolls his head back and forth against the cinderblock.

Lily Chin's classroom is on the second floor in the science wing, across from the science office. When I peer into the room for the first time, it takes me over a minute to pick her out from among the multitude of lounging and sauntering ninth graders. She is the shortest person in the room, less than 5 feet tall, and she is wearing the kind of bright, cotton sundress—with a flounce on the bottom and ruffles around the bib—that young girls wear. When I look closer, however, I realize that Lily Chin is not cute or girlish. Instead, there is a certain tense, impacted dynamism—a serious energy about her—that suggests a presence very much to be reckoned with.

Lily extricates herself from a group of students who have been watching a delicate ribbon snake wind around her hand. "Okay, guys," she says, holding her hand and the snake in the air, "it's time to get started. Today, you'll be working on your Picassos."

"What's a Picasso?" asks a boy who continues to lean against Lily's desk.

"A deformed picture!" calls out a girl to his left.

"Okay, a deformed picture," laughs Lily. "He's not my favorite artist, either. But *you* guys are going to be making some great art today. Now, pencils, paste, boards, and scissors are in the center of the room, reference books are in the back." Everyone scatters.

"What's the assignment?" I ask a girl already at work, dribbling paste on a piece of poster board.

"We're supposed to make collages out of monocots, dicots, and insects. Then identify the genus and species." She reads this information from off the board in a slightly exasperated tone, then shows me a small plastic bag filled with dry grass, a dead grasshopper, and several fluorescent bugs, also dead.

All around the room—between lab sinks, on top of cabinets, in corners on the floor—are cages, terrariums, and aquariums filled with Lily's menagerie of gerbils, white mice, fish, crabs, poisonous and nonpoisonous snakes. An enormous albino rabbit roams freely underfoot, ignored by the students. Above the front blackboard hangs a large, hand-printed sign:

PROCESS SKILLS
1. Observing
2. Classifying
3. Communicating
4. Measuring
5. Informing and predicting
6. Defining
7. Controlling variables

Mobiles of birds and bats hang from the ceiling, and from the walls, map-sized pictures of cross-sectioned fish, grasshoppers, and

earthworms. Earth is Home to Us All, reads one poster of a lion,
Share the Responsibility. Between the ninth graders, the small
mammals, the insects, and the fish, the room is teeming with life, a
kind of Noah's Ark with desks.

"No bug nabbing!" calls out Lily. She is making her way from
desk to desk. "Someone over here said she got a bug nabbed from
her bag! Manners, ladies and gentlemen!" The activity in the room
has grown more intense. From all corners, imploring voices call out
to Lily for her opinion. "Miss, is this good?" "Miss, what should I
do now?" "Miss!" "Miss!" Lily remains unperturbed. She neither
quickens her pace nor attempts to quiet the hubbub that swells
around us. Moving about with her, I feel as if I am swimming in
rough but invigorating waters.

§   §   §

Lily Chin's real name is Fung May, or Beautiful Fairy. Chinese
is the language of Lily's parents and of the country to which she
still feels deep ties. Lily explains her temperament, her values, her
decision to go into teaching, and her interest in biology all in terms
of her psychic affinity to a place where she has never been. There is
something about her that is at once very American and very Chinese. It is the kind of double identity peculiar to those who have
assiduously worked to assimilate, yet are too proud to give up a
cultural heritage they privately feel is superior to the one they have
adopted.

Lily's father arrived in the United States in the early 1920s from
a small village in Canton, in the southern part of China. He had
heard of a growing Chinese community in south Texas, a community originally built from the offspring of Chinese cooks brought
up from Mexico by General Pershing. Forming a partnership with
several other Chinese immigrants, Lily's father opened a grocery
store on the west side of San Antonio, close to where the Mexican
markets now stand. After the death of his first wife, Lily's father
returned to China with his five children and remarried almost at
once. He then made his way back to the United States, where five
more children were born in rapid succession. Lily was number 8.

With other Chinese grocers, Lily's parents formed a merchants'
organization that enabled them to receive credit from wholesale
dealers, an arrangement that ensured plentiful food on the table and
adequate clothes. "We lived in a suite of rooms on the third floor of
an old hotel—multiple bodies to a bed," says Lily, "but I never felt

poor. We *weren't* poor, because my parents really knew how to save. My parents worked incredibly hard all their lives, every day, even Sundays; they never had a day off. There was a powerful work ethic there."

Relations with the Anglo community were cordial, but always tenuous. Lily grew up with a keen awareness of public opinion and of the importance of maintaining a good reputation in the community. "We didn't want to look bad to others. That was very important. That was often discussed. We had to be extra good, and we had to be extra careful. And actually," says Lily, still with pride, "the word got around that Orientals always pay their bills. You never had to worry if an Oriental owed you money. It's part of the Chinese custom: You pay all your bills before New Year's. So people knew — the Orientals would be good for their word."

This same pride and self-consciousness extended to schooling, where Lily was always expected to excel, if only, she says, to prove that Chinese people were good and responsible students. "This was the time, of course, when there was terrible discrimination against blacks here in the South. They rode in the backs of buses; they couldn't go into white restaurants. It was never like that for the Chinese. The discrimination, when it happened, was much more subtle. But it was there, and we learned to be very circumspect."

Even now, as we sit and speak day after day in the cluttered science office at Brackenridge, there is a tense self-consciousness about Lily, a sense that words must be chosen with great care to protect, she says, "not only myself, but my family." Again and again, after telling an anecdote that to my ear seems anything but indiscreet, she says, "Don't print that. You didn't hear me say that."

Lily says that her career was essentially decided for her by a high school guidance counselor. "'You're a smart girl,'" she says, mimicking the counselor's southern drawl. "'You'll make a good teacher.' I really hadn't thought about anything else, partly because there were so few options for women at that time, Oriental women, especially. I just thought, 'Well, why not teach then?' Teachers in China were highly respected people. They were considered extremely important members of the society. That, too, must have been in the back of my mind."

Lily traces her special interest in science back to her Chinese roots — to the grocery store and to Oriental ingenuity and thrift. "In my father's grocery," she explains, "we had octopus and squid and sea cucumbers. He had fish that other people are not interested in using for food. He had all kinds of wonderful and unusual plants that Chinese people eat and use for medicine. And I was exposed to all these things. They interested me from a very young age, because eating was interesting to me. I found everything delicious. Being exposed to all these strange and wonderful things built up a curiosity in me about the world and the way things live and function." When it came time for Lily to select an area of concentration, biology seemed a natural choice.

Having won a substantial teaching scholarship from a local funding organization, Lily chose to attend a small Catholic college in town. The choice turned out to be a good one because the teachers were kind, intelligent, and empathetic. "What I found, I think, by watching those nuns," Lily recalls, "was that a teacher could get the same results from being nice as they could from being demanding; the same results from setting up a comfortable environment as from a tense environment." Ironically, the worst courses, taught by the worst teachers, were the ones required for teacher certification. To this day, Lily resents the inadequate preparation she received and the boredom and waste of those days. "They would give us books to buy, and I thought, 'What a waste of money!' because we didn't ever use the books. We'd use maybe one or two chapters, and that would be it. Absolutely worthless. The only course I remember enjoying was adolescent psychology, where the big, central insight of the course was that teenagers think of clothes as the most important thing in their lives. That was the only piece of information I found useful in my 32 years in the classroom."

Lily's initial interview at Brackenridge High School exposed her to a kind of overt prejudice that she had never experienced before, either in the insulated world of her home or at college. The subtle but pervasive bias that marked the questions she was asked remain etched in her mind. "'Why don't you have an accent?' the administrator asked me, when it was perfectly plain from my resumé that I was born in San Antonio. This guy, this bureaucrat from central office couldn't conceive of the fact that, given how I looked, I could possibly be an American." But Lily swallowed her pride and accepted the $3,000 a year job, joining a science department that had on its staff the only other Chinese teacher in the city of San Antonio.

"The first year was very, very hard," Lily remembers. "I had been given a section of physics to teach, even though I wasn't certified in physics and had had only eight credits of physics in college. I had no experience; I had very little maturity. I had never had any real responsibilities before, and of course, no adequate teacher training. If not for the help I received from my Chinese colleague and from my husband, I would have been in serious trouble." As it turned out, Lily more than rose to the occasion. Within 5 years, she was promoted to department chair.

§   §   §

In second-period honors biology, students mill around briefly before the bell, then make their way to their assigned seats the moment it sounds. All of Lily's classes seem remarkably homogeneous. They are all composed of ninth-grade honors students, almost all Hispanic. In this class, Lily's largest, 26 students sit in a large semicircle at small lab tables, leaving an open stage area around which Lily paces and meanders.

Even before the bell rings, students are shushing one another for quiet, patting the air to signal that the class should settle down to work. This call for silence from a group of ninth graders is an unlikely phenomenon to behold. "We've got a new critter today," says Lily, coming forward with low-key nonchalance. A big, black, ugly-looking bug is wending its way across her hand. "Look at this, guys," she says, "a hissing cockroach!" Several girls recoil, screwing up their faces and screeching. Others lean forward wide-eyed, straining over the lab tables for a closer look. "Listen," she says, with an exaggerated look of suspense. "One, two, three." She clicks the top of the beetle's shell with her finger, and a long hissing sound is heard, like gas through a hose. For a moment the class is perfectly silent. "Now," she says, shaking the bug into a jar, "let's review chapter 16 for the exam." Even as the students open their textbooks to the page, the spell is not yet entirely broken.

The chapter is entitled Arthropods, Econoderms, and Cordata. It looks very dull. "On the test, you'll be required to know the words at the end of the chapter," Lily says. "Why don't we turn it into a game. I'll act out the word, and you try to guess what it is. Number one," she begins, putting her hands up to her cheeks and flapping them back and forth.

"Swimmerets?" someone calls out.

"Swimmerets way up at the head?" says Lily with feigned outrage.

"Operculum!" yells someone else.

"Right! Operculum! What's an operculum?"

"A gill cover."

"All right!" says Lily, and everyone applauds. "Number two," she says, contorting her shoulders back and forth in a spasm.

"Throwing up!" yells a boy in the back.

"That's not a term on your list," yells Lily.

"Molting?" asks a girl.

"All right!" says Lily. And the game goes on.

Everything Lily says in class, every anecdote and piece of information, is perfectly attuned to the ninth-grade sensibility—its
squeamishness, its fascination with disease and the grotesque, and
with sex and violence. "Our crab molted last night," she tells the
class. "Now we can eat it, head and all!"

"Eeyew!" groans the class.

"Arthropods," she says, "have crunchy shells. When you step
on an arthropod, it crunches, like cereal."

"Eeyew!" groans the class again.

"Don't ever step on a dead scorpion," she says in a suspenseful
voice. "The poison is still in the tail. . . . The scorpion kills her mate
right after she's mated. But Mr. Scorpion gets revenge, because the
babies ride around on mama's back and kill *her*!"

"Eeyew!" yells the class. They can't get enough of it.

§   §   §

Lily says that the secret of her success in the classroom is a
mixture of the right temperament and a capacity to adapt over time.
"I was born under the sign of the rabbit," she says. "Rabbits make
good teachers." I must have smirked at this piece of information,
because Lily gets up and begins rummaging through a large box of
paraphernalia—Bunsen burners, torn posters, beakers—and ex-
tracts a rumpled chart depicting the Chinese astrological signs.
"Here," she says. "Rabbits are successful. Rabbits like to show off.
Rabbits attract respect and attention. As a scientist, I used to not
believe in horoscopes. But I do now. Like I believe in acupuncture.
I believe in it because it works. And I believe in horoscopes because
they're so often right.

"I also believe that change is imperative," she goes on. "People
change, life-styles change, education needs to change. So I never do
the same thing twice in the classroom . . . even though I teach five
sections of ninth-grade biology. Every one of them is different, every
day. Every year I make up new experiments for the course. I do
swap shops with other teachers in the department. I'll always try
something new at least once, since even the mistakes, I've found,
are often worthwhile."

Over the years, Lily has experimented with a great range of

programs, especially those that focus on the technique of discovery learning. This is a strategy she always favored, even before it came into vogue. "Biology is a hands-on science, an open-ended science in which there are many variables. In chemistry and physics there are formulas for things, numerical bases for things. Not in biology."

§   §   §

Given her fascination with the new, the unusual, and the peculiar, it is not surprising that Lily's great hobby is collecting. She is the queen of the flea market, the original back-lot scavenger. Receiving almost no money from the school for supplies, Lily has come to rely on garage and warehouse clearance sales for teaching resources. Using small grants and out-of-pocket money, she has purchased a veritable warehouse of junk over the years, most of which is stored in the science office at Brackenridge. This room is filled with the fruits of her weekend forays, from cloth-covered room dividers, to an incubator, to a hulking refrigerator. "From Texas Surplus Supplies," she tells me, "I've gotten the most amazing things: 300 bowling pins at three cents apiece; 300 hardhats, $18 for the whole lot!; $3 for all the chairs in the resource room; $12 for a centrifuge." Lily's greatest find, which she proudly points out, is a large amount of diving equipment, consisting of 22 pairs of shoes, plus hoses, tanks, socks, and ropes—"$35,000 worth of equipment for $150!" I can imagine tiny Lily, in her flouncy cotton dress, backing her truck up to the Texas Surplus loading dock to pick up hundreds of pounds of aquatic gear.

"What will you use this stuff for?" I ask.

"You never know when you'll need a diving tank," she says.

§   §   §

Lily got started doing district in-services when her reputation as a collector (a "resource person," as the principal calls her) started to spread. Though she began with lectures on how to use the seemingly unusable, she soon moved on to topics like classroom management and organization. "I share with the teachers all the tricks I've learned over the years—my numbering system, for example; the way I've learned to number everything I pass out. If I pass things out in order, I can tell which student got which test, and avoid theft. I also tell them how to do different versions of the same test, so that no two students sitting beside each other have the same copy."

Sometimes, Lily tells the teachers, she has to write three or four tests. Cheating is rampant in the school, and students have been known to work out elaborate systems for memorizing test questions, which they sell to later classes. "I lecture the students over and over: Scientists have to be honest; there's no science if there's no honesty. But they still cheat constantly. It's a losing battle."

Part of the problem, says Lily, is that students have changed so much. "Years ago, when I started teaching, most families were intact, even families in the Courts apartments. There was less alcoholism, no drugs. Today, few kids go to church. Few kids learn values at home. They have no social skills except what they get from television. And then, of course, the schools no longer teach civics or ethics like they used to. It's hands-off for the schools when it comes to those subjects. No wonder kids destroy property. No wonder they're rude. No wonder they cheat and steal."

Lily opens her first period class with a cautionary tale. The San Antonio school system holds an aluminum drive each year in which scrap metal and cans are collected to raise money. Last weekend, says Lily, someone stole a dozen aluminum seats from the school's auditorium. Several students snicker at this, and Lily gives them the evil eye. Aluminum was also stolen off a local bridge, making the structure too rickety for use. "One of you could have been killed on that bridge," she says. "Or your mother, or your sister." There is a moment of silence, and then she turns to the work of the day.

It may be that no teacher at Brackenridge High School knows his or her students as well as Lily Chin knows her's, not only because she has been at the school for so many years, but also because she has made a career out of merging traditional classroom activities with the extracurricular. When you take your students on trips, when you sponsor clubs and wash cars with them on Saturdays to raise money, you come to know them in a different way. "When I first started teaching, I mimicked, of course, the way *I* was taught, by frontal lecture. But soon it was clear that with this population, you need to use other incentives — labs and hands-on stuff."

Realizing this, and yet constrained by time and curricular restrictions, Lily started the Lily Chin Science Club, which has evolved over the years into a large, popular, and successful organization. It has been a breeding ground for aspiring engineers, and a refuge for other students who want a friendly place to hang out after school. It is here in the Science Club (recently renamed the Engineering Club) that Lily exerts her greatest influence, instilling values, manners, and discipline taught in the most inconspicuous way. "I get the students as freshmen," says Lily, "so I can sort of sniff out the ones with potential . . . and also the ones who are most at risk. And I say to them, 'You really ought to check out this neat club we've got. We go on trips to NASA. We visit colleges. We enter contests.' Once the kids start coming, I can indoctrinate them. I say, 'Colleges and employers want well-rounded people. Well-rounded people have the advantages, even over MAs and PhDs.'"

In the science corridor, across from Lily's room, a display case features some of the inventions of the Engineering Club. This month it contains a flying machine that placed first in a recent state round of the Physics Olympics, and a collection of sea fossils retrieved en route to New Braunfels, Texas. As Lily explains the origin of each piece behind the glass, three or four students shuffle over to survey the artifacts. What I'm observing, I suddenly realize, is a very subtle effort at persuasion.

"I take these ninth graders," Lily tells me later, "and I work with them continuously in the club over 4 years. And some of them — *some* of them — end up at Rice or MIT or the University of Texas at Austin."

One of Lily's success stories is Sergio, who drops in one afternoon during the last week of school. He is a freshman at Rice, hoping to become an engineer after graduation. Sergio was one of the special students chosen by Lily to act as a lab assistant, a coveted position whose only tangible reward is the right to include it in one's college application.

"Mrs. Chin," Sergio tells me, "is successful with Hispanic students because she shows them she cares. Many of these kids are apathetic and lazy and uninvolved. She gets them motivated; she gets them moving." I ask him what he remembers best about Lily Chin's class. Incubating eggs and then decorating them, is his reply. Collecting bugs. "She has a gift," says Sergio, "for figuring out entertaining things to do."

What Sergio also tells me is that he wishes his high school preparation had been more rigorous. He has had to work terribly hard at Rice, harder than anyone he knows, to keep on top of things. This would probably not surprise Lily, who has been watching her own expectations change over the years, as students seem less and less willing to meet her even halfway. "Recently," she says, "even my best programs aren't working as they once did." Though Lily received special training several years ago to teach Advanced Placement Biology, the students have shown no interest in such a course. And Lily, perhaps sensing the limits of the possible, has not actively encouraged them. It is enough, she says, to get the students to pass, to help them improve their startlingly poor test-taking skills.

§   §   §

On the last day of the grading period, Lily is averaging semester scores while her students work quietly at their desks. "Tell me if you want your grade read aloud," she says. To my surprise, nobody requests that his or her score remain private, nor does anyone express shock or dismay when the grades—51, 43, 48, 70—are read. Even with the automatic 10% that Lily adds to every grade, there are still an extraordinary number of failures.

"It's a terribly frustrating situation," Lily says. "To some extent, the book is to blame. It doesn't target the population well. And the objective tests that go with the text are poor. Their idea of objective questions is different from mine." Next year, Lily and the department will use the text only as an occasional resource. They will make up their own tests and their own experiments, and hope for better results.

The other problem, according to Lily, is that classes are too large to offer the kind of private attention needed to motivate these students. "What's more, we're losing two teachers next year. We're losing them because of a mistake on my part. I saw that we were getting ninth-grade biology students who couldn't read and write at grade level. I went to the middle school and said, 'Don't sign them up for biology after eighth grade. Give them another year to mature.' As a result, the numbers are way down and we're forced to lose one of our very best people. It's a tragedy, and there is nothing I can do about it."

Lily has been department chair at Brackenridge for over 20 years. Though she is a woman, tiny and decidedly low-key in style, her power base in the department has never been threatened. She is also remarkably effective, though nobody can quite define the strategies she uses to create harmony. One physical science teacher refers to her magnetic personality but isn't able to elaborate. Another says only that she is "supportive." Mostly, they tell me anecdotes they know about Lily's classroom teaching, her successes with the Engineering Club, how she parks cars on Friday nights to raise money for school trips, and how she will lend anyone anything she owns, from tests and work sheets to whole curricula. And I realize then that her secret is simply to be a good teacher, a good friend, and to work very, very hard. To be respected for these things is to get your way in others.

Since the passage in 1984 of legislation (House Bill 72) intended to salvage Texas's foundering school system, Lily's role as chair has taken on a new, exasperating, dimension. The bill, like most top-down reforms, has served to create large quantities of mostly meaningless paperwork, while intimidating teachers with restrictive mandates concerning performance and evaluations. "In the new evaluation system," Lily explains, "we have outside evaluators coming in — evaluators who have no understanding of what we're doing. These people are making judgments — uninformed judgments — that actually affect salary. This year is a good example: I had an elementary school teacher coming in to evaluate my freshman biology class. She had no understanding of cooperative learning. Her conception of being on task was entirely different from mine."

Another casualty of House Bill 72 is the school club. New mandates stipulate that teachers will not be compensated for club sponsorship. "What this means, of course," says Lily, "is the end of clubs, the end of after-school tutoring. The end of all those things that build rapport between faculty and students, things that help kids get social skills, that give them a chance to be a leader." Though Lily intends to continue the Engineering Club without compensation, she is clearly resentful. "It's just too bad," she says.

§   §   §

Lily's husband Bob is a policeman in San Antonio. Like her, he is one of only a few Chinese to have entered and succeeded in what has traditionally been an Anglo occupation. He is also a Shriner and member of a Masonic lodge. Lily shows me a photo of her family standing together in their dressiest clothes. They look like the American dream family. Her children are very handsome. As Lily enumerates them, she tells me their Chinese names: Linette, 20, is Snow Cloud; Michele, 18, is Plum Flower; Brent, the baby, is Han Kew, which means Ask Permission of the Heavens.

According to Lily, much of the credit for her relatively easy life, the seamless merging of career and child care, belongs to Bob. He is, she says, "supportive, wonderful, always right. Sometimes I sit around with women of my generation, and we talk about our husbands and how they always know the answer, how to fix things, who to call, and what to say. Bob is very strong; there's nothing he can't do. He was born under the sign of the ox." Bob's talents also extend, it seems, to child care. Himself the product of a large family, he shared equally in the rearing of the Chin children. "Like an ox," Lily says, "he's a workaholic." Still, one difficulty the family has known is money. "With our salaries, it's not always easy to pay the bills. Every time a kid gets sick it's $50. Every time a major expense comes up, it's a crisis."

It is money that is worrying Lily now. Her middle daughter, Michele (honors student, high school valedictorian, and debating champion), has decided to enter Trinity University's five-year teacher education program. When Lily expresses her dismay over this, — "Why couldn't she be a lawyer?" she asks — I assume at first that she is joking. What teacher, lauded by her colleagues, revered by the community, loved by her students, would not want her own child to experience the same rewards? But Lily is too practical and unsentimental to think in those terms. "I went myself to the head of the Education Department at Trinity," she says. "I begged him, 'Please don't encourage my daughter to come to Trinity.' He had basically recruited her. She had had no intention of becoming a teacher until he got hold of her. 'Please,' I said, 'at least give her some scholarship money. Help us out. We're just on that fine line of poverty where we're not eligible for any aid.' And he listened, and smiled, and didn't do anything." Lily sighs. "All that money. And for what? For education courses!"

§   §   §

When I watch Lily teach, I can understand why she feels as she does about education courses. There is nothing in her style, in the easy clamor of her classroom and its purposeful disarray, that bears any relation to what is taught in conventional education courses, at least those she experienced years ago. Everything here seems to derive from an intuitive sense of what is interesting, and an instinctive capacity to balance work and pleasure, restrictions and freedom.

Today she is teaching the respiratory system. Out of 3-liter Coke bottles, tubes, balloons, and rubber bands she has created models of the lung, one per student. "What's the rubber on the bottom represent?" asks Lily, making a slow turn around the stage of the classroom.

"A diaphragm?"

"Yes, a diaphragm. Have you ever seen a diaphragm?" asks

Lily. "This is a diaphragm." She pulls from the clutter of her desk a large tray covered with plastic. Underneath is a half-dissected cat, whose conveniently large diaphragm is intact. The students abandon their lung models and rush to the center of the room. "Eeyew!" "Is that cholesterol in those veins?" "That's the liver! Isn't that the liver?" "That cat had kittens, right?" "Can you eat a cat?" Lily laughs, and answers every question.

Eventually, after poking one another in the diaphragm, and seeing who can hold his breath the longest, and telling stories from the *National Enquirer* about people who sold their lungs to buy bedroom furniture, the students return to their lung models. When the bell rings, they gather their books together reluctantly. "This is an excellent class," says a young man in a matter-of-fact way, as he walks past me. "Write this down," he says. "Mrs. Lily Chin is the best biology teacher in the country." And he is out the door.

5   William Salerno

When I stand outside the door to Bill Salerno's classroom and peer in through the glass window, nobody inside seems to notice. It is late spring, and these are seniors, the same seniors who had been called in for a special assembly earlier in the day to be reprimanded for their tardiness, their distractibility, their alarming senioritis. But at this particular moment, even my stranger's face can distract no one.

Bill Salerno is teaching *Hamlet*. The play lies open on the table in front of him, and he is banging on the page with his fist. His voice is loud and lilting — half Laurence Olivier, half Jimmy Breslin. His free arm, straining the seam of a beige wool jacket, sweeps back and forth. The students' eyes follow his arm.

Bill is talking about Hamlet's mother. "Look at her," he says. "It's easy to hate her, isn't it? She goes off and gets married so fast they can use the same cold cuts at the wedding that they used at the funeral." It takes a minute, but everyone laughs. "She's weak, she's spineless. She's worse than spineless. She's committing incest."

"Just like a woman," calls out a boy slumped in his seat at the back.

"You should know, McDermott!" Salerno shoots back without missing a beat. The class erupts again. "But you know," Salerno continues in a different voice, causing the class to grow grave in response, "she loves her son, desperately loves him. She betrays Claudius after all for the sake of that love. She may be faulted as a wife, but she can't be faulted as a mother." Half a dozen students, including the boy in the back, shake their heads. "So you see, it isn't simple," says Bill. "People aren't simply this or simply that." For the rest of the period, he has them in thrall.

After class, Bill sits at the cluttered desk in his tiny, windowless office at the Winthrop Episcopal School in Manhattan, rubbing his hands together. He is not happy with the class, with what he "did with it" today. "I had an idea," he says. "I had an idea." His hands move in the air as if they are trying to conjure up the ghost of the lost class. "It was all right," he says, "but it wasn't great." Despite 35 years in the classroom, Bill Salerno won't let up on himself. The awards and honors, the honorary degree, the four-inch–thick dossier filled with 30 years worth of letters from admiring students, parents, and colleagues — none of it can set his mind at ease. "I have a tendency to think," he says, "that people don't know what they're talking about when they say my teaching is good."

§   §   §

Bill Salerno is something of a legend in the New York City school system. Survivor extraordinaire, he is an example of someone who has done it all. He has taught academically weak kids and gifted kids, poor kids and rich kids, preadolescents and adults. He has taught English in public and private schools. He has done guidance and college counseling. He has led strikes and reconciled warring factions. And everyone who knows him, whether from Booker T. Washington High School, George Washington Junior High School, Bronx High School of Science, or the Winthrop School, will tell you that he has done these things better than anybody else.

Salerno was born into a family that, on the surface at least, did not seem likely to produce a master English teacher. The son of immigrant parents, Bill grew up surrounded by the sound of another language. "Until I went to high school, I never knew anybody over 60 who spoke English," he says. "As a kid, I honestly believed that when people got to be 60 years old, they stopped speaking English and only spoke Italian!" Salerno has vivid memories of childhood, which he rattles off with the polish and timing of a borscht-belt comedian. Along with his little brother, Bill and his parents shared a tenement flat on 46th Street in Manhattan with his grandparents and two uncles. "There was no privacy," he says. "There was no room to have a thought." Bill remembers scavenging in abandoned lots for broken crates to use as fuel in the family's wood-burning stove. He remembers the one shared toilet down the hall, and the nails from which pages of the phone book or old newspapers would be hung for toilet paper. "Across the street," he says, "was Wilson's slaughterhouse. Summer and winter, I grew up with the smell of death in my nostrils." Sometimes a sheep would get loose and Bill would chase it around the neighborhood, hoping to earn the $5 reward, a kingly sum to a child whose father brought home only $2 or $3 a night as a cab driver. Despite these hardships, however, Bill says that his parents never let him feel poor. There was always food on the table and clothes to wear. "At Christmas," he says, "I would always get a sweater, an orange, and candy from the Kips Bay Boys Club. . . . It was only much later that I realized it was a settlement house, and the Christmas package was for underprivileged kids."

As Bill tells these stories, everyone in the Winthrop teacher's lounge leans in to listen. Everyone is folding up his *New York Times* and grinning. Bill seems somewhat out of place here. In the midst of so much staid homogeneity, he is all ethnicity, broad gestures, and informality. He commands the attention of the faculty room the same way he controls his classroom, through a sense of humor based on a sharpness of tongue that can lighten the dullest moment or level an adversary at a stroke. "I wouldn't *pay* a tie to go with that shirt," he states matter-of-factly to a colleague sitting across from him. Everyone laughs. But when he turns to speak to me again, his changed tone again affects the mood of the whole room. "As a child," he says, "I learned early how to use humor to protect myself." At P.S. 73 and P.S. 59, where Bill went to school, there were sharp divisions across ethnic lines. "Every Monday," he recalls, "all the Italian children were made to line up for head inspection. Only the Italian ones. What was amazing was that they found so many kids with lice. . . . Of course, we all knew it was the non-Italian kids who were the carriers."

Bill's love of literature seems to have been born in him. "I don't remember anyone giving it to me," he says. "It was just something that happened. I would prefer doing that to almost anything. Other kids played sports; I watched movies and read. My mother supported me with the reading, of course. We never had very much, but she thought books were important, and even when I was a kid, I remember her buying little books for me. The library, of course, was my second home. I started young and I just read everything. I'd go to the Cathedral Branch on 50th Street. I used to go through book after book after book. I can remember coming home with four or five different books, and one of the most delicious agonies in the world for me would be deciding which of the five books to start with. To put this one down and save this one for later. . . . Sometimes I read two or three at a time."

This passion was deepened and reinforced at Stuyvesant High School, a public school for gifted children. Whereas before he had looked upon his bookishness and introspection as an aberration, at Stuyvesant Bill found those same qualities exemplified in others. "The books I read at Stuyvesant," he says, "showed me that a lot of the things I'd been thinking and feeling were felt and thought by others. I suddenly saw I wasn't alone. And a good teacher—there were a number of them—could make you see those connections." One of those teachers was Henry C. Davidoff, the author of the *First Pocketbook of Familiar Quotations.* "He was near retirement, an old man, by the time I had him," Bill recalls. "I remember he used to have a lump on the back of his bald head that in the beginning frightened me. Later on, I thought that his brains were trying to get out. There was so much of them." Davidoff was memorable not only for his brilliance, but also for his sensitivity and enthusiasm. "He'd get all caught up in the stuff. I found that very moving, very touching—even then."

Though Bill claims he was born knowing he wanted to teach, it is clear that the example of others, including Davidoff, left a profound impression and made him think of teaching as "a very sacred profession." At one critical moment in his youth, for example, the response of a teacher etched itself into his heart. "When I was 15, my brother was dying of leukemia. He had gradually deteriorated, but in the last stages, that year, he had gone down from 90 to 40 pounds. He had been out a lot in the first half of the term; then from January until June, when he died, he was mostly in the hospital. He was very worried about whether or not he was going to get promoted. . . . So I went to the school and saw his teacher, Miss Howe. She was a lovely lady. I said, 'I'm Robert's brother, and I wonder if I can get his report card.' Miss Howe sat down and said, 'Of course.' She sat down and wrote right down there: 'Promoted to the sixth grade. . . . ' I've never stopped thinking of that."

§   §   §

Bill was drafted in 1950, and his first teaching experience was in the army. Having recently graduated from New York University, he was pulled from regular duty and assigned to teach a variety of subjects, including Commissary Operations, Graves Registration, and Control of Rats, Mice, and Other Vermin. To this day he can rattle off an impromptu lecture on how to use dog tags to prevent choking. He shakes two fingers at me in mock earnestness: "Since the army, I've had a lifelong love affair with the subject of rat extermination. Did you know they can chew through 6 feet of concrete? And they're too smart for poison. You have to keep changing the poisons you use, because those smart bastards catch on and they stop going for it. We lose millions and millions of dollars each year to them. . . . They had a whole damn battery of people trying to outwit them."

Bill's son Robert comes into the office during this story. He leans against the bookcase, his face assuming a long-suffering look, as if he's heard it all before. "My dad, the Rat Man," Robert says, patting his father on the head. At 13, Robert is not only tall for his age (he's the biggest kid in his class at Winthrop), but poised and confident beyond his years. More than once during my talks with Bill, Robert has stationed himself in an armchair and offered unsolicited opinions on various adult matters. He is nearly as glib as his father, with a sense of humor that runs to parody. It is entertaining just to watch Bill and Robert interact, taking verbal jabs at each other until Bill runs out of steam or grows self-conscious.

Bill resisted marriage and fatherhood for a long time. As a young man, he was a free-spirited, independent thinker who is described by one old friend as "the first hippie." Choosing to enroll at N.Y.U. rather than get a job, and to live on his own in Greenwich Village instead of at home, Bill was considered unconventional by his relatives and friends in the old neighborhood. He was also quite a ladies' man, which no doubt contributed to his decision to leave home. "In the area from 44th to 49th Streets," he explains, "if you were seen holding someone's hand it meant you were going to marry her." Bill says he was stupid to have postponed marriage until his mid-40s, especially since he had by then already known for 20 years the woman who became his wife. Though Ann and Bill dated and traveled and shared friends, they held off making their union official. If there is anything Bill would change in his life, he says, it is that.

§   §   §

Immediately after his discharge from the army, in January, 1953, Bill began working toward a master's degree in English Education at Columbia University's Teachers College. He remembers his year at Teachers College as one filled with both frustration and delight. As an English student with a strong interest in philosophy and literature, he was allowed to cross register for many of his courses at Columbia University. There, he studied under such luminaries as Lionel Trilling, Irwin Edman, and Mark Van Doren. When his status as a T.C. student excluded him from officially registering for certain lectures, Bill would sit in on them anyway, blending in with other acolytes crowded at the back of the room.

Bill had somewhat less enthusiasm for his courses at Teachers College itself. Though several proved valuable (especially those in adolescent psychology), he says that the vast majority "lacked sufficient substance to fill a semester." He remembers being driven to the point of frenzy by the inanity of one particular course entitled Supplemental Devices in Secondary Classrooms. "The teacher would sit up in front of the room with these little hand puppets on, talking to each of her hands in a little high-pitched voice. I used to have to leave the room." During the final exam, Bill says he finally "lost it altogether." The assignment was to make a bulletin board. Overcome by a sense of absurdity, he began cutting off pieces of his hair and clothes, and wildly pasting them down on the board. Then he went "running, shouting, down the hall."

After his first semester at Teachers College, Bill and a friend complained to the chair of the English Department, Lennox Grey, about the lack of substance in their classes. In response, Bill was granted an opportunity to enroll in a special no-credit course. "Once a week, Lennox Grey, my friend Stanley, and I would sit around and talk about great books. I found that valuable," says Bill, who is still grateful to Grey for his readiness to admit to the legitimacy of Bill's complaints.

"The basic problem with these ed courses," Bill says of his experience at T.C., "is overkill. There *are* some things that are worth reading, that can help a young person get ready for the classroom. But mixed in with the valuable stuff is so much bullshit, so much filler — things that are self-evident or not useful at all. The whole master's program could have been condensed into a couple of courses."

§   §   §

Bill's first real teaching job started in 1954, when he was hired to teach at Booker T. Washington Junior High School on Manhattan's Upper West Side. Booker T. was a subject school, which meant that the Board of Education considered it a difficult one in which to teach. Teachers who agreed to work at subject schools were given 2 years teaching credit for each year in the classroom. Bill and Ann both spent eight years there, years Bill remembers as among the best in his career. Nowhere else has he had the opportunity to teach students who varied so widely in their abilities. Given the school's reputation at the time, Salerno finds it ironic that some of his best students ever were from Booker T. Washington. But he also encountered there some of the slowest and most emotionally troubled students he has known, and it was at Booker T. that Bill first experienced the frustrating unresponsiveness and general ineptitude of a big-city educational bureaucracy.

Tracking, for example, was an elaborate, confusing system that had been instituted to cope with the great range in student ability. There was a special-progress class for "brilliant" students; there was an English as a Second Language track for immigrant children; there was a program called CRMD for those classified as retarded; and then there was the regular track, which, ironically, was often filled with students weaker than the CRMDs. "The rule was that you had to score at a certain level on the IQ test to be in the retarded program," Bill explains. "When there were kids who scored below, they decided that the solution was to place them in the regular track! So you could turn around and find that if you taught a CRMD class you were in better shape than if you had taken one of the regular groups."

Bill himself seems genuinely to have no preference when it comes to student level. Throughout his career, he has been equally challenged by weak and strong groups. Bill suggests that this impartiality (which he knows is unusual) was bred into him at Booker T. Washington, where he found working with nonreaders to be every bit as rewarding as working with gifted students. With the former, he says, "there were amazing things that could happen very quickly. . . . It was during that period when the Board of Education thought that the way to teach reading was by the whole-word concept, and they were doing that stupid thing with the flashcards, the whole word; I refused to use such a method; I used the phonetic approach. Sometimes over a short period of time I could get kids who weren't reading at all, reading. And seeing their sense of accomplishment, it was unbelievable. In the better classes the kids' ideas could be wonderful, but the change in them was never so visible, so immediate. The weaker kids, too, could be incredibly affectionate and warm, and there was a lot of give-and-take. I loved that."

At Booker T. Washington, that give-and-take extended beyond the classroom. Soon after he began there, Bill was given the additional responsibility of serving as guidance counselor, which, he says, opened his eyes to the real world. "Things happened there that you had to listen to," and as a result, Bill became permanently sensitized to the difficult lives of his students. "One kid would come in and talk about how she didn't want to stay at home because her mother had a new boyfriend, and the boyfriend was making advances at her; or one girl, I remember, she couldn't understand how she'd gotten pregnant because her boyfriend had used Saran Wrap and a rubber band. . . . It would be funny if it weren't so heartbreaking. There was another kid whose mother used to make him dress up in girls' clothing and sleep in her bed with her. Then there was this man who came when we were having trouble with a whole pile of different kids. It turned out he was the father of all of them — twelve different kids with four different mothers — and all of them had different names."

Bill speaks of these incidents as if they happened yesterday. As he recounts one anecdote after another, he names the players by name, including in his telling the kind of detail that memory should have blurred. "Jimmy Lee and I had to grab hold of the index finger," he says of an accidental amputation 32 years ago at Booker T. Washington. "It was lying under the door; then I covered Jimmy's classes while he drove David to St. Luke's."

One of the reasons these memories have remained so vivid in Bill's mind may be that he has shared them over the years with his wife. He met Ann at Booker T., and she knows firsthand about many of the dramas he recounts. A math teacher, Ann shared Bill's counseling responsibilities, often working with him on the same cases. Together they stood on picket lines and battled the same administrators. When they speak, it is clear that years of discussion have created a unity of opinion between them regarding certain colleagues and events.

One person who elicits a violent response from both husband and wife is the department chair at Booker T. Washington who was responsible for Bill's leaving the school. Bill believes that he would be teaching there still had it not been for this "impossible" woman. As Bill describes her, one can see his blood pressure starting to rise. "One time," he recalls, "when I was in the middle of a lesson, she came in and ran her finger over the sill, and wanted me to dust. I said, 'Please don't interrupt my class.' And she said, 'This is a priority. It needs to be done.' The next day, I brought in rags, gave them to her, and told *her* to dust. 'I'm not here to dust and clean,' I said. She didn't like that."

Bill says that this chairwoman drove many people out of the school. But he refused to be defeated by her. "I just didn't care," he says. "I gave it to her. When she saw me coming, she'd lock the door."

This standoff might have continued if she had not gone one step too far. "She changed the principal's ratings on me from positive to negative!" Bill explains. He found this out when the secretary who was typing up the revision informed him in secret. "That lady really hated me," Bill sums up, "and I knew why. Because I had no intention of squatting and pissing every time she told me to. And really, what did it matter to me? I can teach anywhere. Give me a room, a blackboard, a couple of kids, and I'm ready."

§   §   §

From Booker T. Washington, Bill went on to George Washington High, another subject school. He was delighted to find himself working this time for an amiable and sensitive chairman, at a job that proved to be immeasurably easier than the one he had left. "The truth is," he says, "that the worst high school in the world is infinitely easier to teach in than the best junior high." He has come to marvel at veteran junior high school teachers who haven't become combat weary. "They're remarkable people," he says, because their burden is twofold. "Thirteen year olds have so much going on chemically . . . and then there's so much less freedom for a teacher at that level, so much more petty bullshit coming down from the administration."

When Bill talks about his time at George Washington, he speaks in the same superlative terms that he used to describe his experiences at Booker T. Washington. "That was the best class I ever had," he'll say, or "That was the best year of my life." When I remind him that only an hour before he had said the same thing about another class and year of his life, he seems confused and slightly wounded by the observation. "That was great too, but in a *different* way," he says. "It all seems like the best when you put enough space between yourself and the thing. But believe me, there were tears, there were hard times."

But, the hard times seem never to have occurred in the classroom. By all accounts (even his own, though he admits it only grudgingly), Bill has managed to get along with virtually every student he has taught. Though he had some difficult students at George Washington, he does not remember any of them as incorrigible, as ultimately unreachable. "I've been very lucky," he says. "Inside my classroom, at G.W. and elsewhere, it was not difficult. I find it's always hard in the beginning, but by the time you get your class going, the class is never difficult. The kids become *your* kids."

When I suggest that it may not be luck but something he does that explains his success, he says he wouldn't know. "I've had problems with kids. You can't reach everybody. You try, and sometimes you don't . . . but most of the time, you can." He goes on, "Maybe it's a defect in my personality, but I find it very hard not to feel for almost anyone. I think that might be one secret of my success . . . and also one defect. . . . It's like walking up to a baby rattlesnake and petting it because it's a baby. It can kill you. I've gotten involved with these kids' tragedies, their griefs, and it used to almost kill me. But now I'm probably immunized by all those small bites."

As Bill speaks, I remember a story a colleague of his told me in private. "The first days of every year are hell for Bill," she said. "The kids aren't *his* yet, he hasn't yet won them over. And he's so desperately sensitive. He so desperately wants each and every one of them to love him." At the end of the second day of school this year, she said she saw him in the hall, looking grim and ashen. "I put my hand on his shoulder, and it was soaked through to the bone. Like he'd dived into a pool. He cares that much. He's that hard on himself."

§   §   §

Bill spent 5 years at George Washington. Trouble began when the chairman who had hired him retired and was replaced by a new man, "young, vital, but not spectacularly bright," according to Bill. Almost at once, the two began to experience serious philosophical differences. "I was teaching the honors class," Bill says, "and this guy comes to me and says, 'You have to have a floor of 85 in the class. . . . We want to encourage some of the better students to still come here.' What he was doing was prostitution. If you put a kid in the honors class, it meant you were guaranteeing him a minimum of 85, which, at that time, would also guarantee him admission to the city university." When Bill refused, the honors class was taken away from him. "He gave the honors group to a kid, Ed, who'd been the student teacher the term before. Ed was absolutely floundering. He came in every day and I would go over the lesson with him. I'd say, do it this way, do it that way, do it the other way. . . . That was the chairman's job. Eventually, Ed got so flustered, he quit teaching altogether.

"There was pandering too," Bill continues. "The new chairman instituted 'M' classes, modified classes, where the curriculum was absolutely empty. In the past, weaker kids might get watered-down textbooks, or works that were abridged, but at least it was an abridgment of real literature. This went way beyond that. He wanted us to teach the weak kids books like *Marie Goes to a Party* or *The Delco*

Sisters, Beauticians. Now, I said, 'Louis, I'm not teaching *The Delco Sisters*. I've got kids here 17, 18 years old. This is bullshit. I can use a good book and still teach them.' But he said, 'No. We're going to use this wonderful new approach to let the kids know what their community is like.' What he didn't realize was that you could teach what the community was like through the great literature, even abridged. I remember in a shortened version of *The Count of Monte Cristo* there's one section about someone who buries a baby in the garden. These kids told me about all kinds of burials that took place here and there, and abortions. *The Delco Sisters, Beauticians* . . . I mean, really."

§   §   §

Bill Salerno has a deep and abiding skepticism of all educational innovation. He suspects the programs and techniques themselves. And he suspects the people who invent them and the people who impose them. "I know what works best for me," he reasons. "I don't need some goddamn EdD to tell me what to do." Bill's bad experience with *The Delco Sisters* at George Washington High School was not the only time he came to loggerheads over administrative sanctions regarding curriculum. At Bronx Science, for instance, Bill's refusal to comply with an order to submit weekly lesson plans caused a district-wide controversy. When Bill threatened to go public with his complaint the order was rescinded.

"The worst thing that I had to deal with in all my years as a teacher were the rigid requirements for making lesson plans, hitting certain formats, having supervisors who were crazy enough to ask you to underline your pivotal questions in red, and to underline your motivation in blue. . . . If there truly was one wonderful way to plan it would have come up in the past 2,000 years, and we would all be automatically and instantaneously great teachers. You have to suit your lesson plans to your own class, and your own personality, and your own understanding of the material. And it's an art. It isn't a goddamn formula. Half those asses down there at the board who are sitting and making this stuff couldn't teach a decent class to save their lives."

Bill says that he never has, and never will, teach a book that he feels has no literary value. Many times, though, he has taught books he doesn't like. *Demian*, by Hermann Hesse, is a good example. Bill is now teaching *Demian* to several 12th-grade classes at Winthrop. He leafs through a battered copy he has pulled from his attaché case. "This is not one of my great loves," he says, holding the book a little away from him as if it were slightly contaminated, "but I find with books I don't like so much that you can use them to teach certain technique things—like how to trace a symbol or a conceit, how to distinguish shifts in point of view. You don't have to work with every work aesthetically. The way I figure it is, if you're going to have to dissect a book, to kill it, to look at everything—you might as well kill something that isn't so beautiful that you should be arrested for killing it." He laughs. "After a while, you build up a whole pile of important books that you don't like but feel you ought to teach. Then you figure out all kinds of technical lessons for them."

§   §   §

Despite his threats to the department chair at George Washington, Bill had no real intention of leaving the school. When his honors classes were taken away from him, he registered his protest by applying for a transfer that he felt he would never get. "I thought that by making the gesture, and having it turned down, I could save face at George Washington and continue to do what I was going to do anyway." What Bill didn't realize was that his 8 years at Booker T. Washington and his 5 years at George Washington added up to more than a mere 13 years of seniority. Since these were classified as subject schools, each year he had spent in both of them represented two to the Board of Education. With the equivalent of 26 years in the system, Salerno was granted his request of a transfer to Bronx Science, a special high school for the gifted. "I was very unhappy about the transfer," says Bill. "I almost turned it down. I had gotten to be friendly with people I'd worked with, and I was used to my routine." It took a while for him to get used to the change, to the hour-long commute each way and the new staff. But ultimately, he says, "it doesn't make any difference what school you're in, because you close the door with your group of kids and whatever it is you're going to teach takes over, and the relationship with the kids takes over, and the reality is in the room. And the rest of it you can put up with."

Bill's observations about his colleagues at Science are made with a characteristically critical eye. "I got to meet a lot of nice people at Science, a lot of shitheads there too. There were a lot of people who believed the kids were brilliant simply because they were there. There were also a lot of people who got through *because* the kids were good; they would never have made it in a different kind of school." Bill remembers two such individuals at Science who had begun their careers as he had, at Booker T. Washington. One of them had been a hopeless disciplinarian whom the students would lock in the classroom closet every day. Each day, Bill would have to rush into the classroom and let him out. The other one simply couldn't teach and had had the reputation of being "unbearably boring." At Science, though, Bill says the kids were willing to listen to anything. "It didn't matter that he had no personality . . . [that] he was like a human tape-recorder, everyone thought he was wonderful." Clearly this really bothers Bill. "It wasn't teaching," he says. "I shouldn't say that. If it worked for some kids, then it was teaching." But you can tell from his voice he doesn't mean it.

Bill has no patience for bad teaching, which, "more often than not," he says, "means lazy teaching. . . . It's one thing if you don't have the gift, the personality, to reach a class. It's another if you don't even try . . . if you think you can wing it on charm or bullshit." Even though Bill is against the compulsory, formulaic lesson plan, he is a staunch advocate of planning. "I can't stand walking in there and not knowing what I'm doing. I'm not that kind of person. I have in my head an idea of where I'm going. Even if it isn't written down in great detail, I know it goes from here to there to there, and that in the end I want the class to be in this place. There are teachers who think you can go into the class, throw out a word or two, and have the group knock it around like a hockey puck. No one's learning from that."

As Bill speaks, I am reminded of the tremendous control I have seen him exert in his classes, "I often dream that I'm standing in front of the room, and I'm not going to know what to say, . . . or that I'm not going to have enough time, or that I've finished saying what I have to say and there are 30 minutes left in the period." To compensate for that on-going fear, Bill tends to overprepare. "I get more material, and more, and more. I can only relax when I feel completely in control."

Again and again, Bill comes back to his almost absurd perfectionism. Eventually, all the criticism he levels at others is turned against himself. "Teaching for me is always difficult," he says. "I keep thinking, 'I should have done it better; it didn't work out right. I taught the same thing last year in a different way, and it was better.' Sometimes I do that kind of comparing between periods. If the second class isn't as good as the first, I get furious with myself. 'Why didn't you leave it alone? Why didn't you do it the other way?' It's endless."

§   §   §

In Bill's 18 years at Bronx Science, he taught virtually every course in the English curriculum, served on the school's advisory council, and eventually became chairman of the English Department.

In 1982, when the longtime chairman succumbed to AIDS, there was no question but that Salerno would take over the job. During the period when the chairman was sick, Bill not only took over his responsibilities (without pay), but also kept up morale. With no personal interest in the job, he wanted only to keep things organized until the chairman could return. And in the months before his predecessor's death, Bill reportedly put in 12-hour days as both chairman and teacher.

But the 2 years he spent in this semi-administrative position did not result in a hankering for power. After so many bad experiences with administrators, Bill is adamant that the best place for him is in the classroom, not in the office. "If I were interested in management," he says, "I would have gone into management. But I'm essentially a teacher, and I want to teach." Nonetheless, Bill's dossier is thick with letters from the principal at Science testifying to his leadership skills, and to his great contributions to the advisory council and the various curriculum committees on which he served.

Bill sensed that it was time to move on when the position of department chairman formally became his. Fast approaching was the age at which he could retire on a full pension, but it occurred to him that a comfortable position at a private school might be a good alternative to retirement. The headmaster of the Winthrop Episcopal School, where Robert was a student, had come to know Salerno through Parents' Association meetings and fund raisers, and suggested he apply for an opening in the English Department. Four classes of 50 students would certainly represent a radical winding down from the five classes of 150 students that Bill had known for 30 years. Moreover, his pension and salary together would mean a considerable increase in earnings, an increase sorely needed to pay for Robert's school, camp, soccer lessons, piano lessons, and eventually, his college education. Bill applied for the job.

"There was really no way they could turn me down, poor things, even though the powers within the department didn't want anything to do with me." When he arrived at Winthrop for the interview, Bill was treated with a certain condescension. "Here I was," he says, "a big, fat wop with this public school background!" But he was not at all sympathetic to their initial response to him, and he bristles as he recalls it. "I was chairman of the department at Science, I had an honorary doctorate from Georgetown, teaching credentials out to there . . . and they hand me a load of papers and say, 'Here, grade these. We want to see how well you can grade.'" Bill's face reddens.

"One guy asks me, 'How would you teach *Oedipus*?' So I start to talk about the fatal flaw or something, and he keeps shaking his head back and forth, like he thinks I'm an imbecile." Bill came home from his final interview at Winthrop swearing he would never go near the school again. But when the job was finally offered to him, he relented, though he remains sensitive about being an outsider. "A public school teacher will never be fully accepted in a private school," he concludes.

Accepted or not, Bill is now deeply involved in school affairs. "I always have to bulldoze my way in," he says. "It's pathological." Since 1984, he has been advisor to the yearbook, for which he receives no compensation. Since 1985, he has served as the faculty's elected representative to the Board of Trustees. And in 1986, he became form master for the 11th grade, a position that requires him to act as mentor and disciplinarian to about 200 students.

§   §   §

Bill says that one of the major differences between public and private schools is the way each defines teaching. In private schools, where salaries are low, teaching is spoken of as a glorious and sacred "profession" in order to distract teachers from their impoverished circumstances. Public school teachers are less credulous, and define their occupation as a "job." "For Ann and me," says Bill, "there were long periods in our lives when teaching was much less a profession than a livelihood and a job. . . . It's interesting to see that when people want it to be a profession, they talk about lofty ideals and the communication of all these wonderful things to the kids, the benefits to mankind. At the same time, when you're punching a time clock, you can get a notice in your mailbox saying, 'You were a minute late this morning' or 'You punched out one minute early yesterday.' And when that happens, it's definitely a job. Nobody ever sends a note saying, 'You were 3 hours after school giving extra help' or 'You came in 45 minutes early.'"

Throughout their years as teachers, Bill and his wife have both been active in the union. Bill feels a powerful union is critical to teachers' survival. He remembers how, in 1960, he was making $3,000 with incremental raises of $200–$300 a year. "It was the strikes," he says, "that brought about the decent working conditions and gave a little something to teachers. Ann and I were there at the very first strike, when everyone said that it wouldn't work. I remember that one of the big issues was a duty-free lunch period. I thought it was my right to sit down and have lunch, my right to do a number of things that are taken for granted anyplace else."

Bill summarizes his feelings about these early days of union activity: "Most people who come in now don't know what it was like. You just had no rights whatever. It was a very ugly place to be, a world in which the last of the despots reigned. They could be benevolent on occasion, or they could make you absolutely miserable. The union, the hammering out of the contract, the concept of giving teachers dignity—all this came about only when you began to approach teaching as a job and not a profession. Because as a profession, all you got back was a lot of bullshit about how wonderful it was to communicate with the kids, but you still can't have lunch. You have to have certain rights, a place to appeal, you're not supposed to be harassed. You have to be able to know what certain people are saying about you. . . . I say that the things that my wife and I did in the beginning were things we were committed to based on what we knew teaching was all about: You're not only teaching a subject, you're teaching human dignity to the kids. And you can't teach human dignity if you're supposed to kiss ass 9,000 times a day."

Bill first fell in love with Ann (who is still chair of her local chapter) through their union activities. He remembers how, on the day before the first strike, the principal called the faculty into his office and announced that, as he went through their names in alphabetical order, each teacher was to respond by saying whether or not he or she would be present in school on the following day. "People were hesitant and frightened," Bill recalls. "Many of us were permanent subs; we had everything to lose. But when the principal got to Ann, she stood up, put her hands on her hips, and yelled, 'I'll be on that picket line!' What a woman," he says.

Bill has strong feelings about how his home life is connected to his success in the classroom. Having a wife in the same profession (and for some years, when they were not officially married, in the same school) has had a profound impact on his personality, his teaching style, and his commitment. "When your spouse is a teacher," he explains, "you always feel at the bottom line that you're understood. When you have trouble with a kid or an administrator, she knows exactly what it's like." Because Ann taught a different subject and was admired as much as Bill for her excellence in the classroom, Bill never had to deal with either competition or defensiveness with regard to her presence in the school. "We were a support team," he says. "We have always had the same opinions about people, the same gripes. When there's two of you feeling that way, it boosts your confidence."

§   §   §

"There is a tendency," Bill says gravely, pressing down on the spine of *The Death of a Salesman*, "to try to place the blame for this tragedy on Willy Loman." Twenty-six students listen attentively, notebooks open in front of them. For 4 days now, Bill has been working on the play with his second-period juniors. He has lectured on Arthur Miller, on the play's classical and modernist aspects, and on the theatre of the 1940s. Long passages have been read aloud, with Bill taking roles and critiquing the interpretations of his students. The class has been concentrating on the play's central character, the defeated salesman, whom most of the students find somewhat less than heroic.

"You've told me," he says, "that it is all Willy's fault. He should never have cheated on Linda; he should never have attempted to manipulate his son; he should have had more detachment and less ambition. And that's all true. But whenever you're talking about a family, you're talking about a very complex system. You're talking about people interacting with one another in very complex ways. In that kind of situation, it's hard to say that one person is simply the victim and the other is the victimizer, that one is all right and the other all wrong. In a family, on some level, every member of that family bears responsibility for what goes on. On some level, they're all in it together." He flattens the book and looks abstractedly out at the class. "Let's think about that. Let's think about how, for example, Willy's wife Linda might be in part responsible for what has happened here."

There is a long silence. "She's doing the best she can," says one student, defensively. "What's she supposed to do?"

"I suppose she could get a job," says another. "She could insist on working even though that might hurt Willy's pride."

"Yes, she does seem rather passive," says Bill.

"She could have taken a firmer hand with Biff and Happy when they were kids," says another student. "She's too permissive."

The discussion gains momentum. "She could talk more straightforward to Willy," says the student who had defended Linda moments before. "She could encourage him to change jobs."

Suddenly, there are dozens of reasons why Linda is to blame. The class has turned on her, as if obsessed with the idea of her guilt.

"But wait. But wait," Bill interrupts. "What about the sons? Is Biff blameless? Is Happy?" There is a brief pause. Then a new litany of accusations begins.

"The thing I remember most about Mr. Salerno's class," says a former student 10 years out of high school, "is that never for a moment was I ever bored. Never for an instant. I remember sitting in Salerno's class, and over the course of 40 minutes going through a whole range of emotions: laughing hysterically, being really angry, being sad. He could manipulate my emotions better than anyone I've ever known. It was like going to a really great play."

§   §   §

As much as Bill loves teaching, he understands why some have chosen to leave it, and he is well aware of the deprivations one must endure in order to stay in the field. "Economically, it's a tough life," he says. "My kid is going to Winthrop, which is $10,000 a year, and that's only the beginning. The truth of the matter is that, if you're a teacher, there are a lot of aspects of life that are not truly open to you or to your kids. People have left, especially people in math and science, or people who had a background for business. . . . Occasionally, someone moves into law. It's just so lucrative.

"The other thing, of course, is the terrible working conditions. Not just scarce resources and cramped rooms, but dealing with some of the behavior problems in the school. I've been very lucky, but there are people who go in and earn a buck by sweating blood. You can't live that kind of life and do that kind of thing day in and day out. Right now, teaching in New York City is a hard thing. Sure, everyone wants to teach at Bronx Science, but you're not going to get Bronx Science. You're going to go down to one of the 'other' schools. And what happens is what happened to an art teacher Ann and I know. She was bending over, correcting a kid's paper, and someone painted a target on her ass. . . . She took her sweater, tied it around her, and left the school for good; she didn't even punch out. Now, not everyone wants to come in tomorrow and have another target painted on their ass.

"You have to do what's right for you, and many people who moved out were right to move out. If you can't keep your self-respect in this business, it isn't for you. All the people who accuse those teachers of having 'walked out on their responsibility' are sitting in their goddamn *New York Times* offices, typing about 'what this city needs.' The only time those people would even give teaching the time of day was when they were afraid they were going to be drafted, during Vietnam. The minute the draft ended, they packed their asses up and went.

"There is a real difference between teaching in the past and teaching today," Bill goes on. "I remember that as bad as Booker T. Washington was in 1951, 1952, '53, '54 — and there were drugs and alcoholism back then too — you still did have a sense though that if you got the parents in, sometimes, something could be done. I know that it's very different now. There is so much less parental control over the household. Young people are more in charge of themselves than before. It's hard; you either make it or you don't. . . . Now it's up to the school to solve all of society's problems. But the schools just can't do it. Maybe someone will be sensible enough to see that along the line."

One of the greatest stumbling blocks to real teaching, according to Bill, is the burgeoning class size in most schools. "You can't have the same quality of teaching with a class of 35 or more. I know there are studies that say it doesn't make any difference, but that's bullshit. You get 35 nonreaders and nonwriters in a room and you tell me why 35 is as good as having 12."

Not surprisingly, Bill is skeptical of the wisdom of some current educational policies. "The school wasn't built to change society immediately. We are being handed everything: the home situation, the economic situation, the racial situation, the religious situation, the sexual situation."

Bill's skepticism about change has not made him complacent, however. He believes, with current reformers, that standards for both teachers and students must be raised. "I'm glad they're stiffening the teacher licensing exam. It won't guarantee that you have a great teacher, but it will show at least that the teacher is proficient in his subject." As far as student standards are concerned, Bill is in favor of raising graduation requirements, and reemphasizing basic skills. He warns, however, that such drives towards excellence can sometimes backfire. "I do think they have to be careful. Sometimes there's enormous pressure put on people to make the kids achieve at any cost. Then the achievement really isn't an accurate indication of the success of the student. I've heard of cases where people have given tests, standardized tests, on the day when the worst kids were absent from class, so the average will be higher."

Bill feels strongly that the school system has become chaotic and inefficient as a result of decentralization. "Decentralization has brought politics into education in a way that can never be reversed.

Education doesn't live by itself anymore; it's so deeply entwined with politics and interest groups that it's practically strangling itself. Once a system gets this big and this complex, there's bound to be dishonesty, exploitation. More and more things get involved. It's a Gordian knot."

Finally, Bill is convinced that bilingual education is not a means to ensure equal education for all children. He believes that the push for bilingual ed is due, in part, to pork-barrel politics. "I think that if you extend a bilingual program for too long, it's detrimental. It's only by mainstreaming that they get to understand the society they're going to be graduating into. It *is* possible for kids to make it without an ongoing bilingual program. All of us have had those foreign kids, usually Korean or Vietnamese, who sit there with the little dictionary. You talk, and you see those pages rattling, and they're writing everything down. Within 2 months, the kid moves from a non-English-speaking class to a mainstream class and has started to speak not only English, but Spanish as well. Of course, you're dealing with drive there, with motivation. But *that's* what needs to be taught, that it's absolutely critical that English be learned. Otherwise, what happens is what's happening now: we're moving into a second and third generation without strong English skills."

It is late in the day, and Bill has been speaking for a long time. He looks very tired. "Sometimes," he says, sighing his great, tragic sigh, "I feel as if I'm wearing every year I ever taught on my back." Around us is a clutter of ungraded papers in stained manila folders, a half-filled coffee cup bearing a cheerful platitude, and a broken hockey stick that Robert left behind on the desk. Bill surveys the detritus in front of him, sighs again, and begins gathering the stray papers into his briefcase. He is off to a conference about a problem student, then to a Faculty Finance Committee meeting, and finally to a Parents' Association dinner.

"What would you tell someone who was thinking of entering the profession?" I ask.

"I'd tell him," says Bill, "that if you like dealing with kids, with the mind, with literature, then the work is very gratifying. It's very gratifying."

6   Ruth Marantz Cohen

We are sitting in the master bedroom of Ruth Marantz Cohen's split-level house in suburban New Jersey. Beyond the French doors and balcony overlooking her husband Murray's exhausted vegetable garden, the woods are blazing with autumn color. But Ruth is indifferent to the landscape. She sits in her bed, propped up by pillows, coughing at regular intervals. She has pneumonia. This is the fourth day she has been out of school, and the doctor has advised her that at least two weeks of bed rest will be necessary to effect a cure. In Ruth's 30-odd years of teaching in the Morris School District, she has accumulated over 280 unused sick days. It has always been a point of pride with her that she is never sick. And now this.

Throughout the afternoon has come a litany of worries: How will the substitute manage the oral reports on *Candide*? How can anyone figure out her private filing system? Now the French IIs won't get the proper work sheets. Now the French IIIs won't get the subjunctive until December. At 3:00, the replacement calls. "They hate me," moans the beleaguered substitute. "They're desperate for you to come back." Ruth seems calmer. Later, hunched in her bed over a set of homework papers delivered by a neighbor, she tries to explain her excessive concern. "For many years," she says, "teaching was so tied up with my ego that when I wasn't teaching I felt I wasn't fully alive. And even now, though I know I've gotten much better with age, I'm most comfortable in front of a class. *Bien dans la peau* is how the French say it: good in one's skin. Until I started teaching, I never really ever felt *bien dans ma peau*."

§   §   §.

Ruth Marantz is the only child of older parents who fled from Russia to the United States in 1920 to escape persecution. She describes her parents as intellectuals who never had the opportunity to complete a formal education. In their small Brooklyn apartment near Ocean Parkway, the family lived an insulated life, a life that

80

centered mostly around Ruth and her achievements and education. "No one was as interesting to me as my parents were," she says, "and no one was as interesting to them as I was. I remember that my father used to make fun of me sometimes on a Saturday night. He'd say, 'Don't you want to go out on a date instead of sitting around with us?' He knew that I didn't, and he wouldn't have wanted me to."

All the stories that Ruth tells of her childhood are set within the tiny circumference of Avenue C and Ocean Parkway. The stories are so vivid in their detail that in the telling they sound less like memory than fiction: a homey cross between Sholom Aleichem and Marcel Proust. Ruth recounts, for example, the story about the boy, Sonny Bonner, a local delinquent, who drew a slash with his penknife across her brand new pumps; or she tells you about the girl with the enormous nose who was constantly ridiculed by neighborhood children—how one day, someone even drew a chalk picture of her on the sidewalk with a nose that ran around the whole square city block. She can also tell you, in lurid detail, about almost every slight or betrayal or misdeed that was dealt her in the entire course of her youth: the boy who stood her up on New Year's Eve; the cousin who acted aloof at family gatherings.

Ruth's childhood was characterized by close family attachments, but the girl she describes is also one who was easily hurt, and who remembered each hurt as if it were burned into her brain. That sensitivity affected her perception of her parents as well. As deep as her attachment to them was, Ruth was never entirely comfortable with their status as immigrants. In those days, the Marantz's neighborhood was composed largely of poor and working-class Jewish and Italian immigrants. Ruth remembers that outside their own familiar streets, her parents' accents and European ways were embarrassing to her. "I was always aware, even from the time I was a little girl, of people's judgment, their criticism," she says. "And I always felt vulnerable to it because we were different. Immigrants. Jewish. I think my father helped to perpetuate that feeling in me. He used to say, 'No one will help you but your own family. Don't trust anyone but them.' As I got older, I was still conscious of people's judgment, but I also became very concerned with proving my worth to them. It became very important to me to prove to the world that I was superior in some way." Feeling this way, and having neither great beauty nor great talent to afford her easy distinction from others, Ruth says that for a long time she resorted to fantasy; "I remember that I used to imagine all the time that I was other people—Judy So-and-So with the beautiful hair or Ann Something-or-Other who played the piano. I was searching for an identity I could be proud of."

In junior high school, Ruth Marantz finally found the thing that would make her special. "All I remember," she says, "is that a guidance counselor said to me, 'Ruth, next year you're going to be taking French,' and the sound of the word 'French' had this unbelievably powerful effect on me. I didn't even know what French was! I was so provincial, so secluded in my parents' world, that I had only a vague idea that there was a country called France. But I felt my destiny was connected with that word, . . . I really did.

"The next fall," she continues, "I guess I was in the eighth grade, I went to school full of anticipation about this wonderful thing I was going to take. And I remember that during the first 2 or 3 weeks of French class, I had absolutely not the slightest idea of what was going on. I was completely confused. I even remember that first test—on the verb 'to be'—copying the answers off a boy's paper." Despite this slow start, Ruth did end up excelling in French. In high school she won the French award, and then went on to Brooklyn College, where she again distinguished herself as a superb French student. "I had a professor," she says, "a woman named Dr. Harvatt, with whom I had no particular rapport, but who seemed to recognize my special talent for the language." Harvatt entered Ruth in a city-wide French contest, which, to her own surprise, she won. The prize, a summer scholarship to LaVal University in Quebec, "seemed to solidify my identity as a Francophile."

It was during that summer that Ruth first started thinking about teaching as a potential career. "I was never one of those teachers who are born to teach. I had no interest in teaching apart from French." Indeed, the education courses she took on returning to Brooklyn College were, she remembers, "pretty much useless. . . . They were so boring that it was physically impossible for me to retain anything longer than it took to pass an exam. . . . I can't tell you even what the titles of the courses were." Though Ruth received a student teaching post, she was given the opportunity to teach only twice in the course of an entire semester. "The supervising teacher saw that I was nervous, and so he never asked me to take over. I remember 98% of my student teaching experience was spent day-dreaming about clothes. Clearly," Ruth smiles, "my love of French must have been awfully strong for me to go into teaching despite that preparation!"

Scattered about Ruth on the bed as she speaks are folders of papers to be graded, a battered copy of Voltaire's *Candide*, *Profils d'une Oeuvre*, the high class French equivalent of *Cliff Notes*, and then her magazines: *Elle, French Vogue, Marie Claire, Express, Realité.* "This is my hobby," she says, motioning with a broad sweep at the eight or so magazines from which shiny French models smile up at us. She has persuaded the school to subscribe (at considerable cost) to virtually every French periodical available in the United States, and no matter where she sits in the house, an edition of *Elle* or *Marie Claire* is not far away. One finds them in wicker baskets in the den, in every bathroom, on the tea cart in the kitchen, and on the living room endtables. "In my French files," Ruth says, pointing to a dense stack of ragged manila folders near her bedroom desk, "I keep my clippings of ideas. Certain haircuts, coats, a pair of shoes I just love. Sometimes I take out a picture just because it makes me feel happy. It makes me think of France." She leafs idly through a current copy of *Elle* and holds up a photograph of a young woman with a razor cut in a dark brown mini-dress. "Nice," I say. "What style!" she sighs. "The French have such style."

§   §   §

After Brooklyn College and another fellowship stint at Middlebury College, in Vermont, Ruth received a full scholarship at the University of Wisconsin to study for a master's degree in French. She had already met and fallen in love with Murray Cohen, a fellow student at Brooklyn College, who returned from the army to enroll in a doctoral program in chemistry at the University of Missouri. "From the start," says Ruth, "Murray's and my interests were very different. He is the scientist. I'm the humanities person. He's practical. I'm emotional. He's an extrovert. I'm an introvert." But this dissimilarity, evidently, was not enough to keep the two apart. After Ruth finished at Wisconsin, she married Murray and moved to Missouri.

It was at the University of Missouri that Ruth had her first teaching experience — 4 years as an adjunct professor in the Department of French. The experience, she says, was so fulfilling that it ruined her, in a way, for anything else. "Teaching French at Missouri was a revelation to me," she says. "It was the first time I felt really fulfilled, admired, special. Here I was, 22 years old, teaching these GIs — many were older than I was. And I could see I was having an impact on them." Admiration came not only from her students, but from her boss, as well. The head of the department took an immediate liking to Ruth and was immensely supportive. "I remember once he came in while I was teaching, sat briefly in the back of the room, and then announced to the class with great authority, 'Class, I hope you realize how lucky you are to have Miss Marantz as a teacher!' I'll never forget that. It gave me such confidence."

Ruth chose to keep her maiden name, a decision she attributes sometimes to her feminism and sometimes to the fact that she preferred her own name to her husband's. "It's hard to say for certain why I did it," says Ruth. "I think now, in retrospect, that at age 21 the notion of having my name, my identity, taken away was just too threatening." Whatever the reason, Ruth pressed her case to the extent of persuading her husband to adopt Marantz as his middle name. "It was very important to me in those days—and really always—to feel that I was on an equal footing with Murray," she explains. "It's one of the reasons I've always had to work; it's one of the reasons I continued to study. And though the name business didn't last—once the girls were born it became too complicated—I at least had made my point about equality to Murray. At least I'd shown him I didn't want to be squashed."

At Missouri, Ruth began work on her PhD as Murray was completing work on his own. Shortly after she began, however, she became pregnant. When complications set in during the early months of the pregnancy, Ruth quit teaching and began 5 years of a nonworking existence, which she remembers as the most difficult of her life. "No sooner had I fallen in love with teaching than I was forced to stop. I suddenly went from being independent, important, and successful to being confined, fearful. I was dead set on not losing that baby, and living as I did in a fifth-floor walk-up, I was forced to barricade myself in that apartment for 5 or so months. I had no contact with anyone except Murray and the landlady's family. So there I was, taking that poisonous D.E.S. to prevent miscarriage and obsessing about the fact that I was losing my French. 'It's slipping away from me,' I thought. 'I'm never going to be fluent again.'"

§   §   §

By the time the Cohens's second child was born, the family had moved to Morristown, New Jersey, where Murray had taken a job with a small chemical firm. Ruth was into her fourth year of "idleness." With two infants and a new home on an isolated street "in the middle of nowhere," Ruth began to really feel the strain of an uncongenial life-style. "I was not meant to be a mother of young children," she states flatly. "I didn't like it. I wasn't good at it." Tensions that had existed almost from the start of the marriage now worsened. "Again, it was the issue of identity," explains Ruth. "Murray would come home from work and say, 'So what did you do today?' and I would immediately feel very defensive, as if nothing I could say would justify my existence."

After 5 full years as a reluctant homemaker, Ruth accepted the first full-time position she could get, at the local junior high school teaching eight classes a day. "The kids were very difficult, and the work load was ridiculous, but I truly felt as if I'd been reborn. It didn't make any difference that I was only teaching French I, or that Danny Duman fell off his chair every day, or that I was being paid a pittance. I was working! I was talking French! That was all that mattered to me."

In terms of juggling home life and career, the years at the junior high set a pattern for the ones that followed. "I always felt that my teaching had to be the best it could possibly be," Ruth says. "*I* had to be the best. Well, you can't be the best without a lot of preparation. 'Drudgery.' That's what Murray called it. He'd say, 'You've been teaching all these years now; why do you have to go and spend 2 hours the night before rereading the book?' But that's how I had to do it, because it was my ego that would suffer if I didn't do it well . . . And there were plenty of days when I didn't do it well, and I'd feel really lousy about myself. Murray wanted me to spend more time with the family," she continues, "entertaining, cooking more, and doing things that didn't relate to teaching. But to me, teaching French was so imbued in me that I thought about it night and day. God forbid I should have to stay up one night with one of the girls and maybe the next day not go in to teach because I was too tired. I never let that happen once."

§   §   §

In 1960, Ruth was approached by the local high school about the possibility of transferring from the junior- to the senior-high level. Despite the gain in prestige and the considerable reduction in work load that such a move would bring, Ruth was reluctant to accept the offer. At the junior high school, she had tenure and was known and admired. The high school represented uncertainty and the possibility that she might no longer be the best. It was Murray who encouraged her to make the move. "Whatever little conventional ambition I've ever demonstrated over the years has been at Murray's prompting," she points out. "Once he was resigned to the fact that I was going to work, he wanted me to go as far as I could — move to the high school, finish a PhD, become department chairperson. Those were all Murray's ideas. *I* was interested in security. In being the best at what I was doing. In being comfortable."

As it turned out, the decision to transfer to Morristown High School was a happy one. A midsized and well-equipped suburban school, it offered Ruth both security and room to grow. She has now been at Morristown for 28 years, and from the very start she felt supported, understood, and appreciated there. "Maybe I'm an anomaly," she says, "but I've never had any serious problems in my job. Not at Missouri or the junior high or in all my years at the high school. I've had discipline problems, of course; flair-ups with students — sometimes a nasty parent — but never once anything with an administrator." I tell her that her experience does indeed seem exceptional in that regard. "I have, I think, a unique advantage in teaching French," she says. "None of the administrators ever knew French, or any foreign language for that matter. In my first years at Morristown High School, the vice principal Bill Stewart was involved in evaluations. He would open the door and say, 'Hi there!' and that would be the evaluation for the whole period. People used to make jokes like, Bill Stewart evaluates you . . . and he evaluates your legs! In those days, everyone taught the way he or she wanted to, and the administrators just seemed to know who was good." In recent years, of course, evaluations have become more formalized, and even seasoned teachers like Ruth are subjected to them once a year. "I don't mind," says Ruth. "I'm so secure at this point, so used to all that garbage by now, nothing can bother me. In a way it's too bad, but I find the whole evaluation thing amusing. Certain statements like 'Mrs. Cohen used the target language in class' makes me think they don't even know what language I'm speaking."

Although Ruth has always been suspicious of "all the newfangled things" the school bureaucracy is apt to introduce, she is by no means unreceptive to innovation. "All along the way," she says, "there have been people or programs that have influenced me deeply." One of the most important of these was the introduction in 1965 of the Audio-Lingual Method to Language Teaching, an approach that utilizes taped dialogues to teach grammar. She also remembers when the coordinator of language instruction in New York City demonstrated to her department the kind of active teaching that has come to characterize her own style in the classroom. "What he did just made sense. It was easy to apply. It was entertaining."

Finally, Ruth claims to have learned a tremendous amount from every Advanced Placement conference she's attended. "When I first inaugurated the A.P. French Literature course in the mid-1960s," she says, "I was operating entirely in the dark. I didn't even know there was a set syllabus of books that the students were required to read. I remember after the test that first year, one of my best students, Bob Blythe, came to me and said, 'Mrs. Cohen, I think there's something about this course you don't know.' He had scored only a 2 on the exam. Since then, the A.P. conferences have not only filled me in on what's to be taught, but also on how to teach it. I find it very valuable to exchange ideas with other people teaching the same works, to hear what's going on in French classes at other schools. . . . And several years ago, when I launched a new A.P. French Language course, it was especially important to me to be able to get feedback from other places. There was no one in the school to give me any advice."

What *doesn't* interest Ruth is the kind of education talk that goes on at teachers' conventions in Atlantic City. "In 35 years, I've never once attended one of those," she says. "I've never been any good at translating abstractions into practical methods—and that's all you get there: high talk, abstractions, 'what schools need today.' I think it's a waste of time."

§   §   §

Perhaps the greatest influence on Ruth's professional development was a longtime colleague and close friend named Eva Krauss. When Ruth arrived at Morristown High in 1960, Eva was already a fixture in the department, with a reputation as a scrupulous professional and one of the finest French teachers in New Jersey. Ten years older than Ruth, Eva represented for the new recruit both a standard of excellence and a spur to her self-improvement. "Eva fostered in me the healthiest, most productive competitiveness of my life," Ruth recalls. "She was an incredible teacher, unbelievably devoted. I think I can say that Eva was even more attached to what she was doing than I was. And when I saw that—when I saw how good she was, how admired she was—I wanted to be even better and *more* admired. I've always been a terribly competitive person, but in the case of Eva, that competitiveness didn't manifest itself as jealousy, just as a desire to excel." When Eva died, a younger but equally devoted teacher named Jo Foster filled her place. Jo is also a perfectionist, so that productive competitiveness continues in Ruth's professional life to this day. "I've been very lucky in that regard," she says. "I need to be surrounded by people who take their work as seriously as I do . . . and I have been. When you're the only one who's trying, it's hard to keep up your morale."

The third French teacher in the department is a man with whom Ruth has had a less amiable relationship. A Frenchman who has been at the school almost as long as she has, Jean Gautier is guilty, according to Ruth, of a teacher's greatest sin. "He's lazy," she asserts. "He's always *been* lazy. He'll always *be* lazy. In my early years in the school, Jean used to drive me absolutely crazy. I couldn't stand the fact that he didn't take what he was doing as seriously as I did. The students I inherited from him were always ill prepared and turned off to French. But over the years, I've reconciled myself to his presence. We've even become friends. I just don't care as much anymore."

"Jean Gautier has always been Ruth's whipping boy," Murray says later, with a smile that suggests he knows the comment is provocative. "She and Jo love to criticize him." Ruth is sitting across from him, her mouth set in an exaggerated pout.

"You think our criticism is unfounded?" she says in a testy voice.

§   §   §

Ruth's dedication to teaching is based on contrary logic. On the one hand, she states unequivocally that it is *French* that she loves, and not kids or the art of teaching. She is not a woman with a mission, consciously devoted to helping others or furthering kids' development. French language, French culture, French style — these, she claims, are her one and only concern. At the same time, however, it is obvious that Ruth is tuned in to her students. The sigh of one or the smirk of another will invariably draw a comment from her. "I care very much about how the students respond to me," she says. "I want them to like me. In the early years of my teaching, I was *so* tuned in, *so* sensitive, that my feelings were always getting hurt. I would be thinking all the time, 'So-and-so isn't interested in this' or 'So-and-so is angry,' and I'd usually blame myself. I'm much better about that now, but I still do care. It's part of what it means to be the best teacher. You can't be the best if you're unaffected by the student's response to you."

Over the years, Ruth has had a few students with whom she developed relationships of extraordinary closeness. "During the 2 years when my parents were dying, I had a great need for that," she recalls. "My own daughters were in college, and Murray—though he tried—just couldn't fill that need enough. I sometimes think that my teaching, in those years, literally saved my life . . . and the relationship I developed with a particular student back then, Jennifer, was of unbelievable importance to me. She would sit with me after school, and we would talk about the literature, or look through the French magazines together, or talk about relationships. I don't think that now—that ever again—I could have a relationship of such closeness with a student. I've passed through the stage where it was necessary, and I have other interests now. My family, my grandchild, my daughters and their husbands now seem to fill that tremendous need.

"I think you're beginning to see that I'm really an odd case," says Ruth. "I'm not really interested in bettering the teaching profession, but it's crucial that people respect what I'm doing; I'm not really interested in kids, but I want to be the greatest teacher, and that means being really tuned into them—getting them to like me. I'm a loner, but at the same time, I have lots of friends at the school. . . . "

Later in the week, Ruth excitedly calls me on the phone to say that she's thought of another secret of her success. Despite an extraordinary memory for slights, she has no memory for bad experiences in the classroom. "I realize," she says, "that actually, one of the reasons for my success and survival in teaching is that I have no memory from one day to another. Something terrible happens in school—an incident with a nasty kid, a flair-up with a parent—and I'll get terribly upset at the moment it's happening. By the next day, though, it's entirely forgotten. It's gone forever. And I start fresh. I've had unbelievable classes in my career, classes I've called *les animaux*, really crazy kids. But recollected now, they don't *feel* like they were bad. My head tells me they were, but my heart doesn't. I'm angry at kids all the time. But the next day, it's as if they were angels."

§   §   §

Ruth Cohen leans against her desk in a striped minisuit, leafing through notes for a lesson on *Le Mariage de Figaro*. This is French 6, a post-A.P. class she created 4 years ago when several gifted students completed the regular A.P. language class in their junior year. Seven students sit around Ruth in an intimate semicircle, bent over their texts. At 61, with her blond punk haircut, Ruth looks like a contemporary of her students. "Etienne," she says, smiling a sweet, sad smile, "*Avez-vous votre devoir?*" (Do you have your homework?)

"No, Madame," says the young man, disconsolately. "*J'ai eu trop d'histoire.*" One expects her to reprimand the offender, to tell him as other teachers might, that having a lot of history homework is no excuse for overlooking French.

"Ah, *pauvre garçon!*" she says instead. "*Je comprends.* You'll have it tomorrow." And the class proceeds.

From four pages of text from the 18th century, Ruth elicits several lengthy discussions—about menstruation, ménages à trois, Shakespeare's *A Midsummer Night's Dream*, and marital fidelity. "Mrs. Cohen's style of teaching should be called 'progression by digression,'" says a former student. "She taught us how to connect our lives to the literature. Even if we got far afield, and we usually did, we always managed to come away with a good understanding of the work. I've never been sure how that happened."

"I know that my style of teaching is unconventional," Ruth says. "I would never be able to explain to someone how I do it. It's impressionistic. But it works."

§   §   §

Ruth's department chairman is a bulky, good-natured man in his late 40s. He is a Spanish teacher, 25 years at Morristown High, who applied for the position several years ago when chairmanships became formalized as administrative positions. "I'm very lucky," Ruth says, "I have a great relationship with Tony. I did when he was a teacher, and I do now. He leaves me alone. He appreciates me. I think he's wonderful."

As for her own ambitions, Ruth claims that administration has never been one of them. Despite urgings from her husband, she has stubbornly resisted any move out of the classroom. "Part of it was that I didn't want the responsibility of giving advice to other teachers. Since *I* didn't want advice, I couldn't see foisting it on someone else. Secondly, I'm just not a leader. I'm a loner. I like to be left alone in my classroom, with my subject and my students. If I became an administrator, I would no longer be a French teacher! I would have to give up my Advanced Placement classes! I can't imagine that."

Another reason for Ruth's reluctance is political. "I grew up," she says proudly, "with a great suspicion of bosses. My father was a socialist, a union man, and I was imbued, from the time I was a little girl, with a strong sympathy for the worker. As a teacher, I've always been very militant. If there's talk of a strike, I'm with them 100%. I think teachers' salaries are terrible. I think we should be paid a fortune for what we do. If I were an administrator, I'd have to compromise those feelings. I wouldn't be able to walk out. I wouldn't be able to support the union."

Ruth says that male teachers have criticized her militance over the years, given the fact that hers was a second salary. "They've said, 'You can afford to complain. You won't go hungry!' It makes me really angry because the implication is that, just because I have a comfortable life, I have no right to demand adequate compensation for my labor."

Ruth has just finished telling me about her socialist roots, her adventures on the picket line, her deep distrust of the wealthy, when she displays yet another example of her contrary nature: "Go look in my closet," she says. "Look at my new clothes and tell me what you think." Ruth's closet is the size of my bedroom, and is infinitely more organized. On three of four walls hang racks of dresses, blouses, suits. A fragrant odor wafts from the rows of colored cloth. Above these densely packed garments are shelves of shoe boxes, stacked to the closet ceiling, each box bearing a neatly penned inscription describing its contents: "blue sling-backs, 1983" or "high red pumps, 1986." On the opposite wall hang purses, chains, necklaces, scarves. "My new things are in the front!" she calls from the far room. Still sporting their price-tags, a grey dress with a wide belt, a green-and-orange blazer, and a blue mini-dress are stationed like three new pupils in the front row of an exceptionally ordered class. "Beautiful. Beautiful," I say. The clothes, the mirrored dressing area adjacent to it, the cosmetic closet with its trays of eye pencils, lip brushes, unopened Clinique Free Gifts, all remind me of Ruth's claim, that the only other profession she could ever imagine herself involved in is acting. "I'm an actress, and I think you really *have* to be an actress or actor to be a great teacher. You have to love having all eyes on you. You have to be able to play all different roles—sage, parent, friend, policeman—and do it convincingly. You have to have the resiliency to get back on stage after a disastrous performance.

"I've gotten better at it as the years go by. Better at pretending. In the early years of teaching—I think this is true for a lot of teachers—it was hard to stay in character. I used to have problems, for example, playing the disciplinarian. I just had a hard time taking myself seriously when I was yelling at a kid. And the student would know. No, you have to be utterly convincing in your roles, but you have to be able to switch them at the drop of a hat. If you're always playing the ogre, or the nice guy, or the clown, that's not any good either."

When I ask her about other changes in her teaching over the years, Ruth does not mince words. "I won't take any shit nowadays," she says. "In the past, especially in the beginning, I took an enormous amount of shit from kids, arrogance, rudeness. Lately, I'm amazed at how severe I've become, and how easy it is to be that way. I've gotten to see that there are three kinds of teachers: those who ignore disruptiveness and teach in spite of it; those who brook no interference, and the room is like a morgue; and then there's the kind that allows a certain looseness, but nothing beyond—that's the kind I think I am on my good days. In the beginning, I started out in the first category. A lot of talking went on while I was teaching. What would happen is that I'd get so mesmerized by what I was saying that I'd sort of forget about those who weren't listening. At this point, I look at that and I think that's the definition of bad teaching—teaching in spite of what's going on around you. In good teaching, you have to be constantly aware of people's reactions to you so you can change and fit the material to them. . . . In order to do *that*, of course, you have to know your subject inside out. . . . When you're an actor, you've got a script that someone's given you and you've memorized it. As a teacher, the script is your subject and you've got to be constantly improvising on it."

"Ruth Cohen is a consummate actress," a fellow teacher in the Language Department tells me later. He is looking up at the ceiling and smiling. "I've watched her many times over the years. The kids just love it. There she is, all dressed up there like she's going to a party, and she's chattering away in French. She's got so much love for what she's doing, so much respect, that the kids feel it. They're inspired by that."

Both of Ruth's daughters have chosen careers in education, one as a professor of English at Drexel University; the other as a secondary school teacher in New York City and then as a professor of education. Ruth says that it is gratifying, but not surprising, that her girls have followed in her footsteps. "All during their growing up, they saw the perks of teaching—how happy it made their mother, how fulfilled. Murray went through maybe half a dozen jobs during my time at MHS. He had all kinds of problems with bosses, travelling. . . . With teaching, [they] saw I had time to learn and to study. Tenure, too, is a wonderful thing. I'm a person who needs security, and teaching gives you that. But I've come to realize too, that my experience as a teacher isn't typical. And when one of my daughters has trouble—when she is unhappy with her teaching situation, or she feels she isn't getting the classes she deserves, or the kids are rotten to her—I want to tell her, 'Get out!' Because despite everything I say about loving what I'm doing, I know that it isn't the same job now that it was when I started. Kids aren't working as hard. Parents don't care as much. You can be lucky and get a really great situation; but if you're unlucky, and the classes are bad, there's less of a possibility that you're going to redeem them, I think. This kind of thing is the family's responsibility—not the school's, not the teacher's. But nine times out of ten, the family is out of it; they couldn't care less.

"I know it's supposedly a sign of burnout or whatever to say the kids have changed, but I don't *feel* burned-out. I still get up in the morning and think first thing, 'Great! It's a school day! What should I wear!?' I just know that things have changed by comparing what I cover now with what I could cover in the past. With the Advanced Placement curriculum, for example, 10 years ago there were maybe a dozen long novels required on the A.P. list. Over the years the requirements have shrunk. Now there are maybe two or three. Obviously, the Princeton testing people recognize kids just won't do that much work.

"I've tried very very hard to keep my standards high. From French III on, for example, I still won't speak a word of English in class. I know that's not true in most French classrooms. I talk to my classes *as if* they're interested, even if I know they're not. *As if* they're intellectually curious. It's like a game we play. But the quality of their work is so poor, and I inflate the grades more and more because I don't want to demoralize them. I don't want them to give up on French. Already the French enrollment is way down. 'Spanish is easier,' everybody says, so they all flock to the Spanish classes. The kids are still getting into Yale and Princeton and Brown. They're still scoring well on their SATs. They just lack the fire. There are no intellectual students anymore. Just achievers."

To Ruth's great dismay, the recent exodus from French classes is likely to be fueled by the introduction of "critical languages" (Russian, Japanese, and Chinese) into the Morristown High School curriculum. A search is already under way for new faculty to teach these classes, and the French teachers (including Ruth) have been informed that they will be obliged to teach two classes of Spanish next year. "It's typical of the field," Ruth says, "that after 30-odd years of service—refining my skills, becoming really expert in French literature—that they dump two classes of Spanish I on me and say, 'Teach these!' I haven't *looked* at a Spanish book in 30 years, and yet I'm expected to do it, just like that. Nobody could care less that I hardly remember any Spanish. As long as the classes are covered, that's all that counts."

§   §   §

In Ruth's French literature class they are discussing Act II of Racine's *Phèdre*. This is the kind of work that Ruth loves to teach, dealing as it does with unbridled passions and an older woman's lust for a younger man. The students sit in their semicircle, bent over a series of study questions drawn up by Ruth the night before for this one particular class. She is pressing them to expand on their interpretations. "Why? Why?" she keeps saying in French, as each brief response moves the discussion forward in tiny increments. "Tell me more!" she insists. "What do you make of that?" The class displays little energy. "David," she says to a young man with a far-off gaze, "have you ever felt that way about your girlfriend?" The boy blushes, and the class giggles. "You've never felt what Phèdre feels? That kind of longing?"

"No," says the boy. Ruth launches into an enthusiastic diatribe about the nature of love and longing, rushing to the blackboard at one point to write down the French words for love, lust, adoration, and longing. The students copy the words down in their notebooks.

"Sometimes," she tells me later, "I feel their boredom and I can't stand it. When they're bored, I'm bored. That's why I'm so manic sometimes. I want to shake them up. Wake them up. Otherwise, I'll fall asleep."

§   §   §

Despite these complaints, however, Ruth is still an advocate of the profession. "I still do tell my students to go into teaching—to try it. I've been proselytizing for the profession all my life. And to a new teacher I'd say: 'Don't be afraid. Go in with the idea that young people are eager to take from you what you have to offer. Assume

you'll be successful. Lots of times, I think, it's a question of attitude.'"

For many years, Ruth assumed she would teach at least into
her 70s. It is only very recently, with the birth of her first grandchild, that she has begun to reconsider. "It's suddenly conceivable
to me," she says, "that I could live my life without teaching. . . . I
suddenly see that I could remain occupied and be happy without
that classroom. My grandchild — it's unbelievable — is as interesting
to me as my French. Maybe even more. I'm not saying I'm going to
quit tomorrow, but it's something I can conceive of now. And that's
amazing."

On the day Ruth Cohen returns to school after her 3-week bout
with pneumonia, I stand in the hallway outside her first class and
watch as scores of students crowd around her desk, some draping
their arms over her shoulders or around her waist. One girl is actually weeping. "Okay, okay, everybody," Ruth says. "You guys must
really have hated the sub." Then she cocks her head and laughs,
brushes off the toe of one of her green pumps, and begins to teach.

7　Conclusion

Qualitative studies of successful veteran teachers—teachers whose morale and effectiveness have withstood the test of time—are virtually nonexistent in the educational literature. Most of what we know about long-term teachers comes to us through the voluminous studies on burnout. We know from this literature that teaching entails uniquely difficult problems, even compared to other human services professions. The average secondary teacher works with approximately 150 students a day. In no other profession is the professional/client ratio so high. We know that it is one of only a few professions that demand such exclusive work with young people (Sarason, 1982), a factor that makes it especially draining. Literature on burnout also refers to the "isolation of practice" and its long-term hazards—apathy, alienation, and stagnation (Lieberman & Miller, 1984; Lortie, 1975). We know that the structure of the profession is problematic, that weak career incentives can demoralize teachers. Quantitative studies on burnout tell us that over 30% of all practicing teachers wish they were doing something else, and that one in five new teachers will leave the profession altogether (Mark & Anderson, 1978). Finally, there is the question of teacher status and teacher pay.

It is essential, of course, that we hear all this bad news. But when it is presented to us, as it usually is, in terms of cold statistics, it is all too easy to ignore, or to accept it as simply a fact of life. However, when the same facts are expressed by real human beings, it is harder not to pay attention. Case studies can provide a kind of human-interest perspective on the hardships of the educational system as it exists today. In that sense they are very valuable.

But there are other reasons to listen to the voices of veteran teachers. Recent public concern over the quality of teachers, and the great press to improve the profession through policy, have turned successful veterans into valuable resources. It is they who are most knowledgeable about the culture of the classroom, and they who can inform predictions about how teachers are likely to respond to specific policy initiatives. It is they, too, who understand the real needs of students. Public policy need not reinvent the wheel but can instead build on what teachers already know.

What better way, too, to recruit talented students into the profession than by showing them that profession through the eyes of individuals they can respect. No bright young person is going to be influenced to choose a field, especially one portrayed so badly in the media, by platitudes about spiritual rewards. But watching great teachers in action and hearing them speak about the highs of the classroom and the satisfaction of imparting knowledge can have real impact. Teachers like the ones profiled here are not only models of successful practitioners, they are also models of lives that have been sustained and enlivened by a creative commitment to the profession. Andy, Carl, Ruth, Bill, and Lily are proud of their work and have striven against formidable odds to reimagine the teaching profession in ways that preserve, and also enhance, their self-esteem. Despite the liabilities and dissatisfactions that remain part of their jobs, each of these teachers has emerged from 30 years in the classroom with something akin to an artist's pride in his creation. The types of profiles contained in the book may thus be the best possible advertisement for the profession, and may represent our best hope for recruiting other outstanding teachers to replace them.

FIVE TEACHERS, SEEN TOGETHER

I began this study with the assumption that different teachers are successful for very different reasons, and that to acknowledge that difference is to pay homage to the art of teaching. Indeed, though commonalities exist, the individuals depicted in these pages differ markedly from one another in philosophy and personality. One cannot conclude, for example, that any one classroom strategy works best for all five. Discipline, for example, is for Andy a matter of traditional rewards and punishments. For Lily, it is ensured by means of entertainment, a catalog of anecdotes and hands-on activities. Bill controls through humor. The same variety applies to opinions on educational innovation. Three out of the five are deeply suspicious of any form of change. Ruth, Andy, and Bill feel strongly that only they know what is best for their classes, and that nonpractitioners and theorists have little to offer. Carl and Lily, on the other hand, are extremely amenable to change. No conference or workshop is uninteresting to them, and they are themselves frequent leaders of workshops. Neither is there a consensus on the politics of education. While all agree that teachers' salaries are too low, only three out of five believe in the value of collective bargaining.

As to personality, several of these teachers emerge as surprisingly insecure individuals. For them, the classroom is a stage on which they can satisfy their need for praise and attention. Others, like Lily, seem highly confident and free of the doubts that burden Ruth and Bill.

Despite these differences, however, Lily, Carl, Ruth, Andy, and Bill do have certain critical traits in common. Some of these are predictable, while others are surprising. The following is an attempt to define those commonalities, to determine how they came into being, and to analyze how they may function as factors in the teachers' success and longevity in the field.

SUBJECT AS ORGANIZING PASSION

Of all the traits possessed by all five teachers, perhaps the most striking and obvious is the passion each feels for his or her subject. It is a passion that pervades every aspect of their lives, extending far beyond the boundaries of the classroom into speech and habit, hobby and quirk. Bill, for example, devotes every free moment of time to the theater, often attending an off-off-Broadway play on a school night, despite his fatigue. His passion for English literature and drama takes him on yearly pilgrimages to Great Britain, where he can "hear the language spoken correctly" and attend the entire theater season in its first run. Carl's leisure time is spent in his study at home, where he works out mathematical problems on his many computers. Ruth's house is a veritable museum of things French: French magazines, French novels, French provincial furniture.

This passion, it seems, plays a vital role in longevity. Clearly, these teachers' interest in the content of what they teach has served to sustain them when the process of teaching becomes difficult to bear. No intrusive administrator or oppressive state mandate can diminish that enthusiasm. Indeed, in times of stress, all these teachers seem to throw themselves with renewed vigor into their subject. Carl wrote his first book the year his father died; Ruth launched the Advanced Placement Literature course at a low point in her marriage. It is also clear that it was this love of subject, rather than a love of teaching per se, that initially drew these teachers into certification programs. In fact, it was love of subject that kept them on track even when those programs became demoralizing or irrelevant.

The styles of these teachers seem to have developed not out of any self-conscious attempt to apply learned principles of pedagogy, but out of their individual relationships with the subjects they love. As they perceive their subject, so they teach it; as they respond to it; so they communicate it. Teaching style, in short, is a natural outgrowth of personality and predilection. Lily, for example, loves collecting and working with her hands, and these inclinations have become the framework for her teaching style. She has built a pedagogical platform out of her own nature and preference. Bill, on the other hand, is an entertainer. He loves the dramatic inflection and the staged moment and is as effective with his frontal approach to teaching as Lily is with her less conventional methods. Though all these teachers may from time to time nod in the direction of the most current research on effective teaching, their styles remain independent of policy and prescription. "The way I teach," says Ruth, "is a private matter between myself and my love of French. Nothing can ultimately get in the way of that."

TEACHING AND AMBITION:
THE ABSENCE OF GENDER GAP

A lack of concern for conventional career mobility is another commonality among the subjects of this study. It is clear from historical studies of the profession that men and women have long perceived success in education in quite different terms. For men, typically, teaching has not been an end in itself. From early in the century to the present, the majority of men entering the profession have seen the classroom as a temporary way station preceding an administrative job or one outside of education altogether, in business or law. Women, on the other hand, have tended to value teaching for those attributes — the predictable hours, the security of tenure, the freedom to leave and reenter the field without sacrificing status or substantial income — that enable them to strike a balance between home life and career.

Sociologist Sari Biklin (1983) and others have noted that for women teachers, ambition has acquired a unique definition. Whereas men traditionally measure success by upward mobility and rising pay, women teachers turn it into an ideal of self-perfection. They compete not with their colleagues or supervisors but with themselves, as they work to do the same job better and better.

This uniquely feminine type of ambition is clearly apparent in the two female subjects of this study. Ruth turned down the opportunity to become chair of her department, because she felt that such a role might compromise the quality of her work with her students. Lily accepted the position of department chair when it was offered to her, but the focus of her interest is clearly not on administration. Indeed, she is almost dismissive of that role. Like Ruth, she is concerned first and foremost with her effectiveness in the classroom, and like Ruth, her energy is directed almost exclusively to the refinement of her teaching. In short, both Ruth and Lily demonstrate a commitment to their craft that Biklin would call the feminine counterpart to the masculine drive for status and power.

What is even more interesting, however, is that this feminized form of ambition seems to operate in the male subjects of this study as well. The stereotype of the ambitious male teacher is that of an individual with one eye trained on the central office. But, like Lily and Ruth, Andy, Bill, and Carl are all indifferent, even hostile, to the various career-ladder options available to them. Andy and Bill are openly scornful of the administrative route to success. Carl, while less vehement, clearly understands that he is unsuited to it.

Andy, Bill, and Carl also break with the stereotype in the depth of their concern about the quality of their teaching. In different ways, each of these men exhibits a perfectionism every bit as staunch as that of his female counterparts. Bill gets upset every time a lesson he teaches does not live up to his ideal. Carl refuses to use even year-old materials in his classes; he is constantly inventing new games, new tests, new examples. Andy's perfectionism manifests itself in a refusal to capitulate to mediocrity. His standards, for both himself and his students, are unwavering after 35 years.

The absence of the more conventional, "masculine" form of ambition in these men may play a role in their longevity. Given the particular nature of their needs and aspirations, they are not likely to be driven from the field by thwarted ambition, by the disappointment, for example, of being passed over for a promotion. Job satisfaction, in each case, comes purely from within, from the experience of meeting internal standards of excellence that are infinitely renewing.

IN PRAISE OF ORIGINALITY

All the teachers profiled in this study have strong reputations in the schools and communities in which they work. They are known for their commanding knowledge of their subjects and for something equally critical to their effectiveness — their highly distinctive styles in the classroom.

At some point during my visits with all of them, I stood on the front steps of the school at lunch hour and at the end of the day and waylaid random students. "Tell me what you know about the math teacher, Mr. Brenner," I would say, or "What do the students think about that biology teacher, Mrs. Chin?" I expected responses of generic praise, and many of them were. But I was not prepared for the outlandish anecdotes that some students happily poured into my tape recorder, most of them prefaced by such remarks as, "Oh, he's so weird!" or "She's out of her mind!" These comments were invariably made with a curious kind of affection, as if the students were describing an eccentric but lovable family member. What is more, they referred to the teachers with an intimacy at odds with their real experience, since only about a third of the students had actually had the teachers themselves.

The idiosyncrasies that these students characterized as "weird" are the expression of teaching methods carefully crafted to suit the individual styles and temperaments of these teachers. The news of a teacher's originality travels like brushfire through a school. Students remember their grand gestures, their flamboyance, their corniness. They remember teachers with star quality, the ones who seem to always take control of people and situations, if only through sheer drama.

At its worst, such charisma can degenerate into narcissistic showboating, but when it is accompanied by talent, competence, and commitment it can have an exceedingly powerful and beneficial effect. Despite their differences, the five teachers in this study are alike in exercising this kind of charismatic competence. One comes away from all of them with the sense of having met an original. Obviously, this quality is not always necessary for success in the classroom, but it seems worthwhile to acknowledge its effects on adolescents. Often in education, original spirits are regarded with suspicion and disapproval. The more conventional the teacher, the more palatable he or she is to those in charge. The Andys, Lilys, Ruths, Bills, and Carls in the field are seen as prima donnas. And it is true, they are not team players. But their value is not diminished because of this. Instead of imposing sameness on faculties, schools need to recognize what is unique about their teachers and find ways to cultivate it.

THE PERSISTENT NOVICE PERSPECTIVE

Another similarity among the five teachers emerged in the light of studies of career and adult development. The literature that had a particular bearing fell into three categories: studies of adult development per se[1]; studies of career development[2]; and studies dealing specifically with teacher development, including seminal research on moral and ego stages by Lawrence Kohlberg (1976) and J. Loevinger (1976), and research on teacher concerns by Francis Fuller (1969).[3]

What became clear early on, was the degree to which the careers of the subjects of this study failed to correspond to the stages laid out in much of the literature. For example, all the teachers exhibited at least some of the traits associated with Loevinger's (1976) "immature" stage of ego development, which is supposedly attained and left behind in the very first years of teaching. According to Loevinger, young teachers tend to be impulsive and self-protective in the classroom; their primary concern is the avoidance of personal pain and discomfort. Yet Ruth claims that her primary motivation even now is to avoid the discomfort of boredom. "I teach so as not to bore myself," she says, "even if it means jumping on a chair or digressing from the topic for 10 or 15 minutes. I'm very impulsive and spontaneous in that way. I figure that whatever I'm feeling, the kids must be feeling, so I go with my own feelings." Carl, too, explains the changes he makes in his teaching style during administrative observations in terms associated with Loevinger's immature stage: "I do what I have to do to get a good evaluation. When the supervisor leaves, I do what I want to do." In Lily, this kind of novice self-protectiveness shows itself as an almost paranoid refusal to make any remark that might be perceived as a criticism of her administration. In Andy, this youthful perspective manifests itself in his indefatigable energy for battle. With unflagging fervor, he has fought generations of school boards, parents, and administrators. While other young zealots tend to mellow with age, learning the art of accommodation, Andy has remained unyielding.

The majority of teachers in this study appear almost fanatically concerned with the opinions of others, especially their students, another trait supposedly typical of the novice. Ruth claims that until recently she was so sensitive that her feelings were always getting hurt. A colleague observes that Bill is a nervous wreck until he wins his students over. For Carl, the major setback of his career was the rejection of his textbook by colleagues in the school. "It was devastating to me that they didn't want to use my ideas. It was a personal rejection, deeply personal—because my ideas are who I am. And I care so much about [my colleagues'] opinions of me."

These concerns, however, seem to coexist alongside innumerable traits that one would expect of professionals of these teachers' age and experience. They may at one moment express anxiety about discipline or classroom management, and the next speak confidently about the meaning of education and its impact on students over time. Naiveté and wisdom, vulnerability and self-confidence seem to alternate in these teachers continually.

This capacity to retain the novice perspective seems to have afforded the subjects an unusual ability to empathize with young teachers entering the field. All five have been extremely active in championing the rights of new recruits, particularly in terms of pay and benefits. Where such action seemed appropriate, they claimed to be willing to make personal financial sacrifices as a way to boost compensation for young teachers. While their militancy seemed influenced to some extent by regional differences, all five clearly feel an enormous obligation to help new teachers survive in the field. Again and again, they voiced outrage at those injustices of the profession to which new teachers are most vulnerable.

What is perhaps most interesting and surprising about this novice perspective is how its persistence seems to play a role in longevity. By retaining many of the traits of young and inexperienced teachers, the teachers have also retained the urgency and vitality that stave off burnout. There is a vibrantly youthful quality to these subjects, which is manifested in their outlook, their enthusiasm, their politics, and their insecurities. The daily stage fright that many claim to experience motivates them to prepare scrupulously for each class, even after years of teaching. There is no resting on past laurels, no complacency, no jadedness. Every day, it seems, these teachers feel they have to prove themselves again. "The great thing about teaching," Ruth says, "is how every class is brand new. Every class is like my very first class. I start all over again. It's frightening and exhilarating every single day."

SELF-ENABLEMENT VS. STUDENT-ENABLEMENT

According to the prevailing wisdom on the subject, set forth by John Goodlad (1984), Ken Macrorie (1984), and others who have investigated the behaviors of expert teachers, veterans such as these are first and foremost great enablers. Their primary goal in the classroom is to empower their students. Macrorie writes that great teachers "set up dialogues between the experience and ideas of learners and the experience and ideas of authorities" (p. 231). They "eschew lectures" and don't give "conventional tests." Great teachers avoid "frightening learners out of their unconscious selves" (p. 231) Goodlad's (1984) expert teacher makes her classroom a place where students participate in self-directed learning, where she offers a variety of instructional activities and small-group work. Great teachers, according to Goodlad, provide a student-centered classroom.

It became clear early on that all the subjects of this study failed to correspond to these conventional notions about expert teaching. In the classrooms of these teachers there are a lot of frontal lectures and conventional tests. More often than not, these teachers did not avoid, but rather *strove* to frighten their students out of their unconscious selves. Carl seems to speak for all five teachers on this subject. "Some people's mission in life is to comfort the afflicted," he says. "My mission is to afflict the comfortable." Echoing Carl's sentiments, Lily says, "Teaching means the awakening of kids out of their somnolence, even if it means roughing them up in the process."

Finally, the subjects of this study did not run student-centered classrooms. Indeed, though it was not always obvious on the surface, all their classrooms were the very opposite of student-centered — they were teacher-centered. In every case, beneath the appearance of freedom, or even laxity, the central force of the teacher was manifest. In every case, he or she kept an invisible rein on what took place in the course of any class, tightening and loosening that rein with great deliberateness. Even when students freely interacted with each other, challenged the teacher's remarks, or engaged in guided inquiry, the teacher remained the pivotal figure. When there was laughter, it was initiated by the teacher. When there was debate, all waited for the teacher to deliver the final verdict. The teacher was not only the power center, but the moral center as well, the quiet, unswerving fulcrum of authority and wisdom.

When questioned about this phenomenon, which I came to

regard as a kind of benign tyranny, the subjects of this study revealed another commonality. Their responses suggested that the overriding goal of their teaching had little to do with student-enablement. They were concerned, rather, with self-enablement — with getting and holding power. "When I'm in the classroom," Ruth says, "I'm thinking about myself, and the effect I'm trying to elicit in the audience, the role I'm trying to play. If I'm successful, I can feel the audience approval — and that's what it's all about." Similarly, Bill says that he teaches because it gives him enormous pleasure. "I can make every class whatever I want it to be. The classroom is mine." Indeed, in every case, the subject's classroom functions as a kind of stage on which a variety of needs can be asserted and worked through — the need for applause, the need for control, the need for expressing personal talents or interests. Lily turns her classroom into a private laboratory, a place filled with her own collection of toys. Carl finds in his students a captive audience for his humor and boyish antics. Bill finds unlimited affection.

In the case of these teachers then, what Macrorie (1984) refers to as student enablement is merely a by-product of their own pursuit of self-actualization. Consciously or unconsciously, they all seem to believe that if the teacher's needs are satisfied, the students will ultimately benefit.

This is obviously an unorthodox and unsettling proposition for those of us who have always assumed that good teachers must be first and foremost devoted to student learning. The narcissism that seems to be at the root of these teachers' perspective goes against the grain of what we imagine teachers to be: unselfish civil servants laboring for the public good. This image of the selfless teacher has its roots, no doubt, in the very earliest organized examples of our profession — Sunday schools and church-run charity schools. It has been reinforced by the traditional gender structure of schooling. Teaching has been the domain of women largely because it is considered to be an extension of mothering, the consummately selfless activity.

Yet researchers (Cruickshank, 1980; Dedrick & Dishner, 1982; et al.) have long contended that one of the major causes of burnout in teachers is a tendency toward self-abnegation. Teachers are taught that the student comes first. They learn this not only through subliminal cultural messages, but also through teacher education courses and through their experiences with administrators. Years of this kind of psychic self-sacrifice take an enormous toll on a teacher, a toll that can lead to incompetence, depression, and attrition.

It is not hard to see then that a degree of self-involvement is vital to the long-term survival of some teachers. At least to some extent, the subjects of this study have remained invested because they have remained self-involved. To condemn that self-involvement, to legislate against it through public policy, or to ignore its positive ramifications when readying new teachers for the field, is to undermine the very quality on which longevity may depend.

THE CASE AGAINST TEACHER EDUCATION

One of the more distressing conclusions of this study is the subjects' shared estimation of their own preparation for teaching. This subject was brought up spontaneously in the course of interviews by every one of the teachers. It was spoken about with an alarming passion, given the number of years that have passed since these individuals received their training.

In every case, teacher-education courses were characterized as boring, useless, and intellectually demeaning. One of the basic problems, according to Bill, is overkill. "There are some things worth reading—things that can help a young person getting ready for the classroom. But mixed in with the valuable stuff is so much bull, so much filler—things that are absolutely self-evident. The whole semester's program at Teachers College could have been condensed to a couple of courses." Bill is typical of the others when he speaks about the radical discrepancy in rigor between the courses offered by a school of education and those in English offered by a school of arts and sciences. Likewise, Lily remembers an educational psychology course, typical of all those she took, in which memorizing the subheadings of the chapters was enough to earn her an A on the exam.

The rhetoric of education, too, was uniformly distasteful to these teachers. "When I started to get the flavor of what it was like to be in these classes," says Andy, "somehow my English training made me look at that kind of language and that kind of superficial talk as disgusting. It would be like a person who's learned to appreciate Milton trying to get some degree of satisfaction out of reading *Little Red Riding Hood*." Bill remembers "the outpourings of words that pointed to nothing."

The first impulse of a teacher educator is to rationalize away such complaints. After all, the subjects of this study received their teacher training over 25 years ago. At that time, pedagogical jargon was decidedly less self-reflective than it is today. What is more, the 1950s and early 1960s, when these subjects were undergoing their professional educations, was perhaps the most prescriptive and reactionary period in education since the turn of the century. Fueled by cold-war fears and the dire predictions of such critics as Arthur Bestor (1953), teacher-proof curricula and standardized tests proliferated. And teachers themselves, perhaps more explicitly than ever before or since, were perceived as less than central to the educational process.

Since then, the profession has seen the rise of critical-thinking curricula, the adoption of more descriptive and even ethnographic forms of educational research, the movement for teacher empowerment, and the gain in legitimacy of "action research" — all strategies designed to bring the teacher to center stage. But to what extent can the same complaints still be justifiably leveled against teacher-education programs? In recent years there have been clear signs that teacher education has not come as far as it might have. The abundance of alternative certification programs in dozens of states, for example, testifies not only to a shrinking pool of applicants, but also to the deep suspicion of state and local agencies as to the real efficacy of traditional teacher education programs. The increasingly ill-prepared ranks of those who do pass through such programs have been documented in scores of studies. Indeed, the teacher education reform recommendations made by the Holmes Group (1986) and the Carnegie Foundation (1986) address precisely the problems that the subjects of this study complain about most vehemently: the lack of intellectual rigor in professional course work, the overemphasis on classroom as opposed to field-based learning, and the tendency to substitute formulas for problem solving.

Schools and departments of education that have taken these criticisms to heart are constructing teacher training programs that, for the first time, may actually meet the real needs of talented novices. First, they are programs that acknowledge the idiosyncratic nature of good teaching, rethinking many of the traditional prescriptions that have characterized teacher education. The subjects of this study applaud recent attempts on the part of certifying institutions to reduce the required education courses, and to refocus attention on training in the subject that the student plans to teach. They argue that methods courses too often neutralize personality and deintellectualize academic content. What they describe as lacking from their own educations comes close to what Lee Shulman (1986) calls "pedagogical content knowledge," or knowledge of a subject presented as it might be taught, with a sensitivity to the structures of specific disciplines and to the way learners assimilate those structures. Whereas traditional methods courses offer teaching skills devoid of content, and traditional academic courses offer content devoid of teaching skills, pedagogical content knowledge is the necessary bridge between the two. Even these gifted teachers appear to have struggled in the beginning for the lack of it.

These portraits suggest the necessity for other changes in teacher preparation as well. Lortie (1975) concludes in his seminal study of teachers and teaching that "interpersonal capacities" are at the very core of effective outcomes, that style or personality is the key to classroom success. If this is true—and it certainly seems to be for the subjects of this study—then preservice teachers need more opportunities to practice their interpersonal skills in real school settings. Such opportunities provide aspiring teachers with a critical but risk-free testing ground on which to begin formulating a style with which they are comfortable.

IMPLICATIONS FOR PROFESSIONAL DEVELOPMENT

What do the common traits and sentiments of these five veteran teachers suggest about other gifted veterans presently in the field? What should be done with and for them? Researchers and school reformers have traditionally tended to shy away from this population when attempting to bring change into schools, assuming (often rightly, as we've seen) that their habits and opinions are fixed and that they are chronically skeptical and pessimistic. Young teachers, it is reasoned, invariably prove more pliable subjects for the new and the innovative. Rarely do reformers choose the more difficult route of looking behind the veteran's skepticism to discover how it came into being. Rarely do researchers act on the possibility that teachers' wariness is legitimate and grounded in experience.

The field of education has been characterized by a curious kind of ahistoricism—a stubborn refusal to acknowledge anything but the immediate and the new. Since before the turn of the century, curriculum policy in the United States has shifted back and forth between conservatism and progressivism. In the last 40 years, those ideological swings were manifested in the xenophobic Sputnik era, with its call for tougher standards and accountability, and then in a decade of "global education," alternative schools, and humanistic curricula. This, in turn, gave way to a new call for accountability and standards. Teachers like Bill, Ruth, and Andy, who have worked in the schools for almost 40 years, have learned all too well the lesson of such reforms. Indeed, all five teachers speak of the scores of programs and mandated changes they have seen introduced, reviled, and then resurrected in the course of their careers. "How are we supposed to take these things seriously," says Lily, "when everything is outmoded as soon as it arrives? I could save the system a whole lot of money if someone would just ask me in advance if a program will work."

Asking veteran teachers for their opinion is one of the first things researchers and reformers should do. American educational scholarship in general needs to recognize the legitimacy and breadth of teacher knowledge. As J. Myron Atkins (1989) and others have pointed out, recent trends toward acknowledging the wisdom of experience have tended to be superficial. Although researchers have lately begun to include teachers' voices in their work, they are doing so only at the level of data collection. Teachers are still not setting agendas for study; they are still not defining the problems to be examined or the methodologies to be used. Those critical aspects of educational research remain fully within the authority of the university. Yet, as even these five brief case studies show, the interests and preoccupations of the classroom teacher are often wholly contrary to those of the educational establishment, challenging us to widen our definition of good teaching.

What of staff development for individuals like the ones in this study? How can veteran teachers be helped to grow within the context of their own schools and classrooms? Andy and Bill, the most senior of the five subjects, would probably say that they do not *need* to grow. In-service workshops and conferences have nothing to offer them anymore; they have already found the right measures and the right techniques. Experience has led them there.

It is hard to disagree with this argument. Indeed, it is difficult to imagine that any conventional in-service workshop could bring to the attention of these teachers a method or strategy they have not already considered. It is ironic that contemporary education, which is so preoccupied with learning styles and individual differences among students, perceives the needs of teachers to be so uniform. For example, the staff development opportunities offered to veteran teachers are invariably the same as those offered to the newest recruits. Rarely is experience or expertise acknowledged in such sessions. No one, it is assumed, knows more or less than anyone else.

Instead of subjecting veteran teachers to in-service presentations that they will inevitably resent or ignore, and instead of dismissing the veteran as impossibly closed-minded and curmudgeonly, schools would do well to tap into the rich store of their expertise, using them to teach newer faculty members about the nature of good teaching and survival. Many of the traits these teachers possess in common—their sensitivity to the plight of the novice, for example, and their capacity to identify with novice fears and uncertainties—make them ideal mentors for new recruits. Passion for subject, perfectionism, strategies of self-protection and self-enablement are all valuable qualities and lessons that are not taught to student teachers in their preservice programs.

Indeed, if effective changes are to be made in preservice education, the input and active involvement of veteran teachers are imperative. Teachers like Andy, Bill, Lily, Ruth, and Carl should not only be the subjects of study but also an integral part of the faculty in teacher education programs. These master teachers should be encouraged to teach methods classes and design teacher education curricula. The involvement of such teachers in these programs would be of benefit to education students and would also provide teachers themselves with an opportunity for meaningful professional development. Defining and articulating the classroom philosophies that have governed their careers would encourage them to examine those philosophies in ways they have not done before. What is more, their involvement in the teaching of new recruits would give them a way to enhance their careers without leaving the classroom. Andy, Bill, Ruth, Carl and Lily all claim that not once in the course of their long careers were they ever asked what they do and why. To ignore such expertise is unacceptable. We must begin to enlist the support of those who can help us best.

Notes

1. The studies that I found most suggestive for the purposes of this research were those of Erikson (1980, 1985), Levinson (1978), and Sheehy (1976). All three see human development in terms of a series of discrete stages or cycles, characterized by a central conflict. Erikson's theory of the "epigenetic cycle" was particularly apposite to the subjects of this study. According to Erikson, individuals move through a series of eight developmental stages from infancy to old age, carrying with them as they grow vestiges from previous stages, which serve to gradually delineate an increasingly complex personality. This notion of interrelated stages, with traits from youth carried into old age, corresponds markedly with the behavior and beliefs of the veteran teachers observed for this study.

2. Another approach to the study of adult development is that of career development. The work of Donald Super and Douglas Hall (1978) illustrates the thrust of this literature, which focuses on the decision-making aspect of career and the way in which choices create personal life patterns. Super's five stages of career development begin with a period of exploration, in which interests, expectations, and limitations are defined and integrated. Next come the stages of "trying out" (ages 25-30) and "establishing yourself" (30-45). By age 45, according to Super, the individual is at a pivotal point in his or her career, where growth, maintenance, or stagnation emerge as the three options that will determine later life. Between ages 45 and 65, many individuals reexamine their professional choices and make critical, long-postponed changes. The final stage, of preparing for retirement, involves a winding down within the professional sphere. Priorities are reevaluated yet again.

Super and Hall draw various conclusions about the nature of the teaching profession based on its relationship to these generic stages. Teachers advance through the first three stages more quickly than do those in other professions, and as a result, a teacher's professional reputation is established very early in life. Of several conditions contributing to professional growth over time, two seemed particularly germane to this study. An initial high degree of job challenge tends to stimulate teachers to perform well, both in the beginning and in subsequent years. A high degree of job autonomy and involvement encourages them to take responsibility for their success or failure.

3. Lawrence Kohlberg's (1976) theory of moral-judgment stages sees

human beings as progressing through a series of ethical phases. In the first, "pre-convention," stage, we act morally out of fear of punishment; in the second, "convention," stage, we behave morally to gain the approval of others and out of concern for the social order. It is only in the last, "post-convention," stage that our behavior is predicated on what is just and principled. Individuals move through these stages at their own pace. Very few achieve the highest moral condition early in life, and many never achieve it at all.

Loevinger (1976) defines similar stages of ego or self-development. Teachers begin at an "immature" ego level, where their primary concern is with the avoidance of personal pain or discomfort. At the next stage, they tend to be concerned primarily with conformity, with following school rules and codes. At the last level, individuals become self-conscious and scrupulous. Here, self-imposed prescriptions dictate behavior. Teachers at this highest level of moral development strive for personal meaning and self-consistency—the cornerstones, according to Loevinger, of "character formation, interpersonal relationships, and self-conception" (1976, p. 7).

Perhaps the most important work in the study of teacher development is that of Francis Fuller (1969). His "stages of teacher concern" lays out a four-level continuum through which teachers pass in the course of their careers. These stages—preservice experience, "survival," the "teaching situation," and the "mature" stage—trace the shifts in teacher preoccupations in the classroom. The mature stage, which all the teachers in this study should have reached, is when professional capacities are fully developed. Here, according to Fuller, the teacher's focus is primarily on student concerns and student needs. Instruction and discipline are individualized, and the overriding interest of the teacher is the quality of his or her rapport with students, parents, and administrators. At the same time, the need for popularity diminishes. The teacher may become interested in the history and philosophy of the profession. Outside interests and family relationships also take on greater importance at this stage.

References

Atkins, J. M. (1989). Can educational research keep pace with education reform? *Phi Delta Kappan, 71*(3), 200–205.

Bestor, A. (1953). *Educational wastelands: The retreat from learning in our public schools*. Urbana, IL: University of Illinois Press.

Biklin, S. K. (1983). *Teaching as an occupation for women: A case study of an elementary school*. Syracuse, NY: Education Designs Group.

Carnegie Foundation Task Force on Teaching as a Profession. (1986). *A nation prepared: Teachers for the 21st century*. New York: The Carnegie Foundation.

Cruickshank, D. R. (1980). *Teaching is tough*. Englewood Cliffs, NJ: Prentice Hall.

Dedrick, C., & Dishner, E. (1982). A secondary teacher's view of teacher burnout. *Clearinghouse, 55*, 417.

Erikson, E. (1980). *Identity and the life cycle*. New York: Norton.

Erikson, E. (1985). *The life cycle completed*. New York: Norton.

Fuller, F. F. (1969). Concerns of teachers: A developmental characterization. *American Educational Research Journal, 6*, 207–266.

Goodlad, J. (1984). *A place called school*. New York: McGraw-Hill.

Holmes Group. (1986). *Tomorrow's teachers: A report of the Holmes group*. East Lansing, MI: The Holmes Group.

Kohlberg, L. (1976). Moral stages and moralization: The cognitive developmental approach. In T. Likona (Ed.), *Moral development and behavior: Theory, research, and social issues* (pp. 31–53). New York: Holt, Rinehart, and Winston.

Levinson, D. (1978). *The seasons of a man's life*. New York: Knopf.

Lieberman, A., & Miller, L. (1984). *Teachers, their world and their work: Implications for school improvement*. Alexandria, VA: Association for Supervision and Curriculum Development.

Lightfoot, S. L. (1983). *The good high school: Portraits of character and culture*. New York: Basic Books.

Loevinger, J. (1976). *Ego development*. San Francisco: Jossey-Bass.

Lortie, D. (1975). *Schoolteacher: A sociological study*. Chicago: University of Chicago Press.

Macrorie, K. (1984). *20 teachers*. New York: Oxford University Press.

Mark, J. H., & Anderson, B. D. (1978). Teacher survival rate: A current look. *American Education Research Journal, 15*, 378–383.

Sarason, S. B. (1982). *The culture of school and the problem of change.* Boston: Allyn and Bacon.

Sheehy, G. (1976). *Passages.* New York: Bantam Books.

Shulman, L. S. (1986). Those who understand: Knowledge growth in teaching. *Educational Researcher, 15*(2), 4–14.

Super, D. C., & Hall, D. T. (1978). Career development: Exploration and planning. *Annual Review of Psychology, 29*, 333–372.

Waller, W. (1932). *The sociology of teaching.* New York: Russell and Russell.

Index

About the Author

Rosetta Marantz Cohen is an assistant professor in the Department of Education and Child Study at Smith College. She has taught at Teachers College, Columbia University, and at Trinity University, and spent seven years as an English teacher in New York City high schools.